ADVENTURES IN THE AFRICAN JUNGLE

Mary L. Jobe Akeley

1933

By Mary L. Jobe Akeley

✦

CARL AKELEY'S AFRICA

CARL AND MRS. AKELEY WITH THE SAMBURU
WOMAN, BILLY-BILLY.

ADVENTURES
in the
AFRICAN JUNGLE

By Carl *and* Mary L. Jobe
AKELEY

With Illustrations

NEW YORK: DODD, MEAD & COMPANY

1932

32410

To Mother

SARAH JANE PITTIS JOBE

who has given lavishly in effort, in sympathy and in understanding and who has continued to possess throughout the years the courageous and invincible spirit of youth,

THIS VOLUME
IS LOVINGLY, GRATEFULLY AND
REVERENTLY DEDICATED

FOREWORD

One of my cherished memories is of evenings, during several summers, when Carl Akeley and I sat together on the quaint rear porch of a certain club in the heart of Manhattan. Lofty walls, that seemed to lean askew, rose all around. One would look in vain for a sprig of foliage or an inch of soil. But above, in a cubistic frame, was a portion of sky as deep and ineffable, even if not as clear and sparkling, as ever hung over the jungle. In that aloof and usually lonely court, my friend told me some of the tales that I find reborn in this volume.

Mary L. Jobe Akeley, fellow worker with her husband during his final campaign, and heir to the responsibility for fulfilling his purpose, has edited the field notes kept by the great explorer-naturalist from the date of his first African expedition during the 'nineties.' The stories from manuscript sources and those from the lips of her husband have been discriminatingly mingled with many of their joint experiences. Moreover, every reader will recognize and enjoy the observations that are peculiarly feminine, in the sense that few men would realize the importance of recording them. In this category I place especially the intimate details of camp life, the preparation and serving of food on *safari*, the relation of mistress

Foreword

and servant in Africa, the well portrayed personalities of black boys who are really the foundation of any African undertaking.

We who read this book gain a new insight into the personalities of animals as well as of men, and we see vividly some of the anomalies that arise when nature and civilization collide. (The rhino and the locomotive did that literally.) We see giraffes, with sublime unconsciousness, mowing down telephone wires in the African war zone, and thus committing the crime of preventing Europeans from shooting each other. We see elephants tobogganing down a mountain slope on private landslides. We find, in dour Somaliland, the beast that was the unicorn, and are almost made to see him with the imagination of our remote ancestors.

In another connection I once wrote that the explorations of Carl Akeley in his beloved Africa were inspired by a passion that his fellow men might henceforth be enabled to catch glimpses of the peerless wild life of that great continent as if through his own fortunate eyes. Mary L. Jobe Akeley is continuing the realization of that dream.

ROBERT CUSHMAN MURPHY

American Museum
of
Natural History
August 11, 1930

[viii]

PREFACE

When Carl and I began our African journey in 1926—his *fifth* and my own *first* in that 'Bright Continent'—it was our intention to write together the story of our expedition. But it was in the land of his dreams that he was called to undertake the greatest of all adventures, which, I trust, I too may face with equal courage, fortitude and unfaltering trust.

Now that my account of his last and most important expedition, CARL AKELEY'S AFRICA, has been published (1929), I am presenting this new volume in order to fulfil Carl's hope that we might do an African book together and to tell in simple narrative form the *truth* about certain animals and natives in that astonishing and, to most people, still remote country.

Carl Akeley loved children passionately. He seldom considered his work so important but that he would interrupt it in order to satisfy the inquiring interest of the young visitors who frequented his studio and museum work shop. He delighted in telling them of the life habits of animals and in explaining the processes of his taxidermy and sculpture. This love of children we shared completely from the beginning of our friendship; in fact it was perhaps not so much my early explorations in the mountain wildernesses of Canada as

[ix]

my work in the training of girls in the out-of-doors that first aroused Carl's interest in me. Realizing as we did that the accomplishments of tomorrow are wholly dependent upon how the minds of our young people are trained today, it was to both of us, not only a service of devotion but a great joy to make some lasting contribution to the eager child whose acquisitive and imaginative impulse drives him to learn the facts about the beasts and peoples of strange and far away lands. Therefore, for boys and girls still in their teens this book and also another volume which will be published later on have been primarily designed.

Here I have assembled stories which my husband delighted to recall and to relate to friends both young and old. Other narratives I have compiled from the field notes of his early expeditions not hitherto reproduced. To these I have added chapters recounting adventures which we shared as well as a few of my own experiences when, after Carl's passing on Mount Mikeno in the Belgian Congo, I completed his unfinished work.

For permission to use certain material in Carl Akeley's IN BRIGHTEST AFRICA, I am deeply appreciative of the kindness of Mr. Nelson Doubleday, of Doubleday, Doran. I am under obligation to *Boys' Life* for the use of extracts from a series of articles my husband wrote for that magazine. I am also grateful to Charles Scribner's Sons and to the Roosevelt family for the privilege

[x]

African Jungle

of reprinting Theodore Roosevelt's *Joys of Africa,* which my husband considered a classic.

I am indebted to my secretary, Virginia Deering, for her care in the mechanical preparation of the manuscript copy; to Sam M. Jones for his work in arranging diary material, particularly that in the Somaliland chapter; to Sophie DeNeen and to Kent B. Stiles, for assistance in proof reading; to my old friend Dr. Benjamin W. Mitchell for helpful criticisms; to Dr. and Mrs. Richard Travis Atkins, who generously placed at my disposal their Ridgefield country home in whose peace and quiet I was enabled to write a considerable portion of this book.

It is my sincere desire not only to give my readers a few happy hours when they may project themselves into our life in a remote land but also to portray with fidelity, its strange peoples and its stranger animals. If this volume inspires an appreciation of the fast vanishing wild life and of the rapidly changing native of a romantic and alien land, if it conveys a more friendly notion than is usually conceived of the Equatorial regions of that Bright Continent, then I shall not have tried in vain.

Mary L. Jobe Akeley

American Museum
of
Natural History.
September 1, 1930.

[xi]

CONTENTS

[xiii]

ILLUSTRATIONS

[xv]

Illustrations

Chapter headings from drawings by A. A. Jansson

[xvi]

ADVENTURES IN THE AFRICAN JUNGLE

CHAPTER I   ELEPHANT

BY CARL AKELEY

HUGE gray shadows are creeping through the forest but there is not even an echo of a footfall. The feathery foliage is stirring overhead. But there is no sound. You are only dimly conscious that something is happening in the great mysterious jungle. Something is living, breathing, moving vaguely, in the awesome gloom. A faint whisper—"Tembo!" The black gun boy has seen! His eyes are a hundred times keener than a white man's will ever be. Cold steel—your heavy gun barrel—is slipping through your cold fingers. They shake a little as you grasp your rifle and bring it to your shoulder. Suddenly you are face to face with the greatest mammal in the world. The elephant! Free and fearless, quick and powerful almost beyond comprehension, he fixes his small wicked-looking eyes upon those who have dared to cross his trail. With ease and grace his long, prehensile trunk, so near and so menacing, may reach out and smite, finishing an earthly career forever. The herd has been disturbed; it stands tensely silent, while the scales of life and death balance and a coin spins at the feet of the gods.

Now, with scarcely a murmur, the great elephant herd shifts and ebbs and flows. It has seen you, but the dawn breeze has been favorable. Tembo has not smelled you. He glides noiselessly into the inner recesses of the great dark forest. The lord of the land has spoken and his word is 'peace.'

The sun breaks through a piled up cloud, its rays filtering through the tree tops to the trail beneath. A tiny bird twitters—bursts into song high up on a moss-draped bough. The silence is shattered. Something relaxes the whole length and breadth of your nervous system. Tembo has retreated to the remote feeding grounds of his jungle home.

*   *   *   *   *

The elephant always may be trusted to provide the hunter with plenty of excitement. His great size, colossal strength and magnificent courage are qualities that make him stand out as one of the most interesting as well as one of the most dangerous of beasts. Often he appears when least expected and frequently does the totally unexpected. Walking unprepared into his presence is like stepping out of a quiet home into No Man's Land—it

Photo. by Carl Akeley.

ELEPHANT HUNTING IS A GAME FULL OF EXCITEMENT.

Taxidermic mount & photo. by Carl Akeley.

THE ALARM:—THE STORY TOLD BY CARL AKELEY IN HIS TAXIDERMIC GROUP OF ELEPHANTS IN THE AMERICAN MUSEUM OF NATURAL HISTORY.

Adventures in the African Jungle

may be perfectly safe but the odds are considerably against it.

One day in Uganda we followed the trail of two old bull elephants for five hours. We were in a big feeding ground and the elephant tracks crossed, intermingled and circled in a bewildering maze. I had told Bill, my faithful Kikuyu gun bearer, to follow the trail, more to test his ability than in the hope that he would succeed in bringing me to the herd. But I underrated Bill. Suddenly the boy stopped short and held up his cane as a signal for caution. Not more than twenty feet from us stood the two old bulls. They had not heard our approach nor had they caught our scent, but as I studied them from the shelter of a dense bush I realized that we were in a very dangerous position.

I had no desire to kill an elephant, except one for my museum group—and that meant only an unusually fine specimen; but I had even less desire to be killed by an elephant. So, with two of them as close to me as if we had been in the same room, and with nothing between us but a flimsy screen of bushes, I could take no chances. I hesitated, trying to convince myself that the tusks were fine enough to justify a shot. Then, without warning, my decision was made for me. A great gray trunk was thrust inquiringly forward—forward until it nearly touched my gun barrel. The movement may have been an attempt to catch my scent. I do not know. I had one glimpse of

[3]

angry eyes set in a solid wall-like head—and I fired. The animal, wounded in the neck, swung around and bolted. I could not watch him nor gauge the effect of my shot, as his companion was right in front of me. He paused for a moment; then, apparently familiar with the deadly language of the rifle, he made a quick retreat.

Bill and I followed for about a hundred yards. The wounded bull scented us, turned and charged. I took aim, but there was no need to press the trigger, for the giant had made his last stand. His column-like legs swayed, crumpled beneath his weight, and the tremendous body lay outstretched on the ground. My bullet had pierced the jugular vein—a quick death. It had been a chance shot but, fired from such a short distance, it was much more effective than such shots usually are.

I had luck that day. Not, however, until some years later, when I talked with other hunters in Nairobi, did I realize how good my luck really was. I talked with men there who had had experiences similar to my own but who had not had my good fortune in escaping without injury. Great hunters who had been tossed and trampled —and lived to tell the tale.

Outram by keeping cool in a great emergency saved himself from a most unpleasant death. He had shot an elephant and the beast had fallen. Believing it finished, Outram approached. "Suddenly," he said, "to my surprise and horror the *dead* elephant rose and rushed at

[4]

me. He caught me with his trunk and I went spinning through the air. I don't know whether in that brief flight I thought at all, but by the time I landed rather hard in the grass, amazement had given way to fear and I was sure that something had to be done and done quickly.

"I could see the elephant coming after me to trample me into the ground. Fortunately he paused for a second to crush my helmet, which had fallen off during the attack. That second saved me. I got under the beast's tail and there I clung while he wheeled and circled in a vicious attempt to get me in reach of trunk or tusks or feet. After a few moments of this sport, my injuries began to tell on me. The unequal contest could not have lasted much longer. Fortunately at the crucial moment my companion arrived and killed the elephant."

Hutchinson's story was similar to Outram's. An elephant caught him in the same way, wiped up the ground with him and then threw him into the trampled vegetation; but he had presence of mind enough to mix himself up in the animal's legs until his gun boy could fire.

The angry beast that caught Alan Black more nearly carried his charge to a finish. The method of attack was the same; but when the elephant discarded him, Black landed in a bush that broke his fall. The elephant followed and stepped on him, returning two or three times to step on him again, but the bush into which Black had fallen served as a cushion and saved his life.

Adventures in the African Jungle

The elephant's trunk is the most remarkable organ any animal possesses. The arm of a man is notable because it may be swung about at any angle from the shoulder, but the elephant's trunk may be twisted and turned in any direction and at any point in its entire length. It is just as powerful in one position as in another. It is without bone—a great flexible cable of muscles and sinew, so tough that the sharpest knife will scarcely cut it. It is so delicate that the elephant may pluck the tenderest blade of grass, yet so strong that he may lift a tree weighing a ton and toss it about easily. With his great height and short, thick neck, the elephant would find it difficult indeed to feed if it were not for his trunk. However it enables him to secure the choicest morsels on the ground or in the tree tops and to strip a whole forest of bark and branches, if he feels like it. With his trunk he has a most extraordinary ability to detect the faintest scent and to punish or kill an enemy.

Since the elephant has something like a fair chance, elephant hunting, unlike a good deal of the shooting that is done in the name of sport, always seems to me a legitimate game. This splendid animal wields a pair of heavy weapons—his mighty tusks—each one of which may weigh as much as the average man; and they are backed by several tons of brute strength. With an agility and a sagacity not to be rivaled by any other beast of his size today, he is a worthy opponent for any sportsman.

Adventures in the African Jungle

Elephant hunting is always a game full of interest and excitement, because the elephant is such a wise old fellow that the hunter never learns all of his tricks.

Swiftly and surely the white man and the white man's rifles are getting the better of old Tembo. Everywhere is he compelled to retreat before the advance of civilization. But occasionally the African elephant has his innings; and when he does, he winds up the episode with a dramatic flourish of trunk and tusks that the most spectacular handling of a gun cannot rival.

Every elephant hunter has known moments of nerve-torturing suspense—moments when his wits, his courage and his skill with a gun have stood between him and an open grave. His opponent is adroit, fearless, resourceful, and possessed of tremendous strength. Of course, no one can put himself in the elephant's place and imagine the animal's feelings when it faces a rifle, but I am convinced that this great beast's attitude is one of supreme confidence. A man is handicapped, when he confronts a charging elephant, by his own state of mind. He knows he has 'picked the fight.' He knows he is the intruder. And he has a guilty feeling that creates in him a demoralizing fear that could never affect one who enters a contest with an absolute conviction of right.

"Here's something about half as big as one of my legs," says Tembo to himself. "A dwarfed thing equally objectionable to my eyes and nose. He's trying to frighten me with that little stick he's carrying but I'll trample the runt and gore him and perhaps sit on him afterwards."

Then, when the 'stick' emits a roar and a flash, if death is not instantaneous, the elephant is thoroughly angered and becomes more dangerous than before. To the hunter it is a different story. He is not overconfident, through ignorance of his antagonist's power. Instead, he is handicapped by the knowledge that if his gun or his wits or his nerves fail him he will be quickly finished by the charging beast.

If the man keeps his head, he has slightly more than half a chance in any combat with elephants; but if the elephant gets his man, it is fairly certain that there will be no need for the services of a doctor. There are exceptions to this rule—once in a while the victim survives—as I can testify.

I had been on a collecting expedition for the museum, and had obtained all the necessary specimens, when an old bull who tried the quiet waiting game 'got' me. Descending from the ice fields of Mount Kenya, that snow-capped peak on the equator, we had made a temporary camp, intending to rest until our base camp could be portered to us. The interlude gave me an opportunity to make some pictures of the typical elephant country all about us. With a party of fifteen, including gun boys and a few porters, I went back up the mountain to an eleva-

Adventures in the African Jungle

tion of nine thousand feet at the edge of the dense bamboo forest.

Probably all would have gone well, and I might have obtained some valuable photographs, had we not run across the spoor of three large bulls. It was an old trail and I knew it would take time to follow it, but the tracks were so unusual in size that I could not resist the temptation. There was always the chance that the trail might be crossed by a fresher one made as the bulls circled about feeding, but instead it led us on from noon until sundown without bringing us to any new sign.

The night on the mountain was so bitterly cold that we were glad to be up and on the move again at daybreak. There was frost in the air and the morning was still misty when we entered a great elephant feeding ground. It was an open space where the rank growth attained eight or ten feet in height and where the animals milled about eating the vegetation and trampling it down until there was very little left. The place itself was a labyrinth of trails, and from it, as the spokes of a wheel radiate from a hub, were the clear and definite tracks of the departing elephants. Soon after we left this feeding ground I came upon the fresh tracks of my three old bulls, so fresh that they must have been in that very spot an hour before.

But the network of paths led nowhere. For some time we wandered about in an attempt to follow the elephants;

[9]

then, growing impatient, I left the clearing, intending to circle about it in the hope of finding on its outskirts the trail which the tuskers had taken. I had gone but a short distance when I found more fresh tracks. I stopped to examine them, and, as I did so, the crackling of bamboo not two hundred yards ahead caught my attention. The bulls were almost within rifle shot and were giving me the signal for the final stalk.

I waited while one of my trackers ran silently along the trail to a point about fifty yards away where it made an abrupt turn. He indicated the direction the animals had taken. Then I turned my attention to the porters, watching them select a place to lay down their loads in a clump of trees where they would be somewhat protected in case of a stampede. The second gun boy presented his rifle for inspection. I examined it, found everything in order, and sent the boy to a safe distance with the porters. The first gun boy presented his gun; I took it, handing him the rifle I had already examined. The second gun was now ready. I leaned it against my body and stood, my back to the wall of the forest, blowing upon my hands numbed by the cold and chafing them in order to have at a moment's notice a supple trigger finger. At the same time the first gun boy was taking the cartridges from his bandolier and holding them up so that I could be sure that each was a full steel-jacketed bullet—the only kind that will penetrate an elephant's head. There was no reason to suppose that the animals suspected our presence, and I prepared for the stalk with my customary caution and with more than my usual deliberation.

I was standing with my gun leaning against my hip, still warming my hands and still looking at the cartridges one after another. In a flash, one of the calmest moments of my hunting experience changed to the most profoundly intense moment of my entire life. I suddenly *knew* that an elephant was right behind me. Something must have warned me, but I have no idea what it was. I grabbed my gun, and as I wheeled around I tried to shove the safety catch forward. It would not budge. I wanted desperately to look at it, but there was no time. I remember thinking that I must pull the trigger hard enough to fire. Then something struck me a staggering blow. I saw the point of a tusk right at my chest. Instinctively I seized it in my left hand, reached out for the other tusk with my right, and went to the ground between them as the great body bore down upon me. One merciless little eye gleamed savagely above me as the elephant drove his tusks into the ground on either side of me, his rolled-up trunk against my chest. I heard a wheezy grunt as the great bull plunged forward, and I realized vaguely that I was being crushed beneath him. Then the light went out.

It was evening before I recovered consciousness, in a

dazed sort of way. I was dimly aware of seeing a fire. I was lying where the old bull had left me, in a cold mountain rain, while my superstitious black boys, believing that I was dead, refused to touch me. I tried to shout, and I must have succeeded after a fashion, for a little later I felt myself being carried away by my legs and shoulders.

Later I had another lucid interval, in which I realized that I was in one of the porters' tents. Then I tried to piece together the events that had led to my accident. I supposed that my back was broken because I could not move. I felt no pain. I was miserably cold and numb, and that reminded me of a bottle of brandy, carried for emergencies. I ordered the boys to bring it to me and pour it down my throat. I also had them prepare for me some hot bovril, and gradually the numbness left me. Then I discovered that I could move my arm a little. I tried the same experiment with my leg and was successful. Though the effort brought pain, it told me that I had at least a chance for recovery.

When morning came, my mind was clear enough to inquire for my white companions at the camp below, and the boys told me that soon after the elephant knelt on me they had dispatched a messenger asking for help. At that rate, assistance should have been close at hand. Fearing that the rescue party was lost on the mountain, I ordered my heavy gun to be fired every fifteen minutes, and within an hour my boys heard an answering shot from a smaller rifle.

When relief arrived I was a sorry looking spectacle. The blow from the elephant's trunk which had stunned me had also skinned my forehead, blackened and closed an eye, broken my nose and torn open one cheek so that my teeth were exposed. Several of my ribs were broken and my lungs were punctured. I was covered with mud and splashed with blood. But apparently it was my face that was the awful sight.

Just why I was not crushed completely, I shall never know. Beneath the old bull's weight, or even under the pressure of his enormous trunk, my body would have offered about as much resistance as a soda cracker. My only explanation—and I think it is the correct one—is that a root or rock under the surface of the ground must have stopped his tusks, and that seeing me unconscious he must have thought he had killed me. He had then left me and had charged about the clearing after the black boys.

My experience is just one more illustration of my idea that a combat between a man and an elephant is still a fairly equal contest. Even the express rifles of the twentieth century have not given the hunter an overwhelming advantage over this mighty beast.

There is no older game on earth than that of elephant hunting. Before the dawn of history, some twenty thousand years ago, the elephant's claim to aristocracy among the hunted things of the world was well established. At that time his ancestors, the mammoths, clad in heavy hair a foot long, were common in western Europe. Often their portraits were painted and carved in outline on cavern walls in southern France. Even then the contest had begun, as is clearly proved by charred and broken mammoth bones found among the relics of cave men. Fifteen hundred years before the time of Christ, Egyptian kings recorded in hieroglyphics the number of tusks brought home from elephant hunts.

In the days of Alexander the Great and of Pyrrhus, Indian rajahs were training elephants for use as beasts of burden and as war steeds. In modern times the taming of the African elephant is in its beginning. A small herd of elephants, however, trained to work, is found in the Belgian Congo. This herd, now efficient in lifting and in hauling is a tribute to the patience and skill of its trainers as well as to those who conceived the plan.

The heavy work of timber hauling, as in India where elephant power is so valuable, is not everywhere a factor in Africa because of the scarcity of the forests. The great beast can be used only in areas where there is ample forage. His appetite is enormous and in Africa, the regions of plentiful feed are by no means abundant. From time immemorial brown-skinned natives have trapped old Tembo for his flesh and for his tusks, and ivory hunters

Sculpture & photo. by Carl Akeley.

THE WOUNDED COMRADE: ELEPHANTS MAKE A SUPREME
EFFORT TO ASSIST A COMPANION IN DISTRESS.

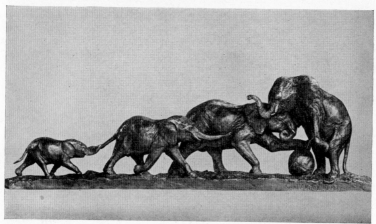

Photo. & bronze by Carl Akeley.

LITTLE ELEPHANTS PLAY AT JUNGLE FOOTBALL.

Photo. by Carl Akeley.

ELEPHANTS IN THE WILD ARE A COMBINATION OF
ANIMATION AND POWER.

of every nationality have followed his trail and even to-day are tracking him into the remote parts of Africa. For many years to come he will probably be considered more valuable for his ivory than as a beast of burden.

Man has not played this elephant hunting game for centuries without learning at least its elements. There are many white hunters in Africa who have gained great knowledge of elephants, and it was with one of these professionals, Cunninghame, that I did my first tracking. He was a real hunter, and he taught me everything that one man can teach another about the game; but even so it did not take me long to discover that my schooling had only begun. Most of the essentials in hunting an animal as intelligent as the elephant belong in the list of things that can be learned only by experience. He who can understand the elephant well enough to guess his next move—and then forestall it—will stand the best chance of success.

Moreover, there is much to learn about an elephant in addition to the best method of killing him; and learning it gives one many a thrill. An elephant alive is vastly more interesting than an elephant dead, and my object in going into Africa was not primarily to kill, but to make acquaintance—as intimate acquaintance as possible with the live, wild elephant in his jungle home. I have studied Tembo for months at a time under every possible condition; on the plains, in the forests, on the mountain sides, even above ten thousand feet—and I have reached the conclusion that the professional hunter has missed half the excitement, half the interest and half the sport of his own game. I firmly believe that of all the wild animals on this earth today, the African elephant is the most fascinating and the most difficult to understand.

The student of animal nature must know how to handle his elephant gun. Frequently when he least expects it he is forced to use it. The great expanse of hide of an African elephant would seem to make him as easy a mark as the proverbial barn door. But as a matter of fact there are only three vulnerable points in all his huge body. You can kill if you can hit an elephant's backbone and sever the spinal cord. You can kill by hitting his brain or his heart. A bullet anywhere else probably will not hurt him much; at least, not immediately. But the brain and heart shots are the only safe bets. I say 'safe' a bit doubtfully, for the brain is armored by an amazingly thick skull, and the heart in silhouette would cover only an approximate square foot of area; and, besides, it requires a good knowledge of elephant anatomy to locate it in the huge frame.

It might not be so difficult to place a shot in one of those three assailable spots if elephants were not so clever at playing hide-and-seek. Elephants in the jungle do not exhibit themselves from trunk to tail as they do in the circus. You are lucky if you realize that the little patch of gray hide showing through the foliage is not a section of granite boulder, and if you can distinguish an old cow's motionless trunk from the surrounding trees.

The elephant is so nearly the color of the shadows and the tree trunks and the boulders that he may be as invisible as a cotton-tail rabbit in a hedgerow. The point of a glistening tusk, a sparkling, wicked little eye, or the tip of a great scalloped ear, is not camouflaged as successfully as the trunk or a patch of hide; but even with such a starting point it is a picture puzzle. It will give you more serious thought than entertainment to figure out just how the beast is standing and where one should aim among the bushes to strike heart or brain. Failure to select a vital point may be fatal to the hunter.

A bullet from an express gun which hits an elephant in the head will not invariably stop and turn him. One time when I was coming down through Uganda I crossed the tracks of a herd of elephants. As we were down wind from them and as it was about noon, the quietest hour of the day, the chances appeared good for overtaking them with ease. It seemed an excellent opportunity to look them over and perhaps to find the big bull I needed for my museum group. Just as I expected, we approached unnoticed to within twenty-five yards. We examined them leisurely through the glasses, as they gathered in the shade for their usual siesta. I have never seen African elephants lie down. They come together to rest, mill lazily about under the trees, and only occasionally change position. We studied the slowly shifting herd, taking our time for it and finding it almost as difficult to select a particular elephant from the mass as to distinguish his outline behind a screen of shrubbery.

At last we picked out what seemed to us an exceptionally fine bull. One of the party took deliberate aim and fired. The elephant dropped, apparently dead. We could not rush in for the customary finishing shot, for, instead of making off with all speed as is usually the case, the herd lingered. To our great surprise when his companions finally got under way the bull struggled to his feet and continued after them. A volley of bullets from our guns appeared only to speed his departure.

We followed the elephant, taking his own trail because the vegetation was too dense to travel silently in any other way. We had been going for some time, hoping to reach a space sufficiently open for us to leave the trail and come alongside for a more effective shot. Suddenly I began to realize that the trail had been slowly turning so that the wind was from us to the injured bull. Hastily we moved out to the side, but we were too late. The bull already had our wind. I knew he had it, although I could not see him, for there was a crashing among the bushes as he wheeled. Then came the piercing scream of an angry elephant.

No one who has heard that scream ever forgets it.

Adventures in the African Jungle

It is like a shrill locomotive whistle, intensified by the consciousness that the locomotive is after *you*—just *you*. It is the warning of a charge, and after it echoes through the forest a man who knows what it means needs plenty of self-control not to fire wildly. Snorting and grumbling our elephant now broke through the underbrush. Gun in hand, I waited. On he came, bursting into view, with his great ears outspread twelve feet from tip to tip and his trunk thrown high and furiously lashing the air. At thirty yards I shot. He stopped, but seemed puzzled rather than hurt. I emptied the other barrel of my rifle and signaled to my gun boy for the second. Shot after shot I pumped into him with as much effect as if I were firing so many bullets into a mountain wall.

Meanwhile my companion had been shooting also, and with equally unsatisfactory results. We were frantically wondering how to gain time to reload, when the old bull answered the question by retreating into the woods. Obviously he wanted a moment's breathing space away from the pelting rain of bullets. All the rules of elephant hunting seemed to have failed. We had fired numerous shots, several of them well placed brain shots. The first should have turned him; and, failing that, any of the others should have killed him. But he had taken them, and finally gone off seemingly unharmed, leaving us weak, bewildered and absolutely helpless.

Scarcely had we reloaded when we heard him coming

on his second charge. Screaming, grunting, roaring, he rushed at us. Again the first shot stopped him. Again he took our fire standing and finally retreated, angry but apparently no worse for our barrage. It seemed we could not knock him down. What, then, if on his third charge we could not even stop him? I was sick of it and quite ready to quit, but we had started something that had to be finished. He now came at us so promptly that we had no choice but to stand our ground. For several seconds we could hear his onrush without seeing him. Then he came into view, headed some thirty feet to one side of us and thrashing the limb of a tree back and forth in his trunk.

Without stopping to wonder by what lucky chance his charge should have been so utterly misdirected, I fired once more. It was a good brain shot, this time from the side, and it took quick effect. The old fellow tottered and fell lifeless.

A second later a trembling native crawled out of the bushes in front of our dead bull. It was my tent boy, Ali, who at that moment was the whitest black boy I have ever seen. Without my knowledge he had followed to watch the sport and had experienced the supreme fright of his life when, luckily for us, he happened to draw the last charge. When I examined this elephant I found the thickest skull I have ever seen. Almost any of my shots would have killed an ordinary animal, but in his case all but the last—the one fired from the side—had been stopped by bone.

Another animal who tried to hunt the hunter by doubling on his own trail was the old bull which now forms the central figure in the group of African elephants which I mounted for the American Museum of Natural History in New York. He also proved to me most effectively that the elephant has another advantage over man in the hunting game—the ability to move through the forest as silently as a shadow. I had wounded the beast, but he was still leading me a long chase. I followed one hour, then another, and finally settled down for a good long trek in country where the going was rough and the forest too thick to see in any direction. Suddenly, with no warning whatsoever, the elephant charged directly across my path. I fired two hurried shots as he passed, and he disappeared in the growth on the other side of the trail. He was tired of being followed, and had come back after me, intending to wind up the affair in his own way. The inaccuracy of his charge probably was due to the fact that he was depending on sound to locate me rather than on sight or scent. It was a close call—the elephant was less than ten feet away when my shot stopped him, as I afterwards proved by placing the skull at the normal height and extending the line cut through the bone by my bullet to a point at the height from which my gun was fired.

High up on the Aberdare Range, where the slopes are so steep that a horse can travel only with the greatest difficulty, but where the elephants move along with an amazing ease and rapidity on age-old paths worn deep in the rocks, a herd of elephants, whose spoor I was following, again got my wind by redoubling on the trail. Realizing that they were passing me as they descended on a parallel trail, I gained on them by cutting across at my own level. And then I learned something more about the sagacity of elephants. They came to a place on the mountain where it was so steep that a landslide started beneath their feet. All around, the earth was soft and slippery. As each elephant reached this spot, he squatted, remaining perfectly motionless as the loose dirt gave way beneath his tremendous weight. One after another the tuskers tobogganed down the mountainside as if *glissading* on a snow field. One by one, as their respective mud sleds came to a standstill some two hundred yards below, they got up, shook themselves and proceeded on the downward trail, leaving me high and dry and safe above them.

Now that my elephant-hunting days are over, and my specimens of the grandest beast of the Bright Continent

Adventures in the African Jungle

are mounted in two great museums of the Western World, I like to think of the elephant not as my enemy but rather as an honorable and worthy opponent who is so placed in the grim scheme of existence that at times he has sought my life as I have sought his. I have never killed except for scientific purposes or to save myself from death. The elephants I have seen in action require no apology—they have always been moved by the instinct of self defense.

I like to think of the elephant as a member of a clan to which he is intensely loyal. I like to think of him as a creature of tremendously keen intelligence and of lively sympathy for his kind. I like to recall the way the young and husky members of a herd form an outer defensive ring to protect the very small and the very old when danger threatens. I like to remember the efforts I have seen elephants make when lifting up and helping along a wounded comrade. I like to visualize the splendid struggle the elephant has carried on throughout the ages and the versatility he has shown as he has adapted himself to changing conditions and has defended himself against varying modes of attack, each more fatal than the one before. Finally, I like to think of the obstinacy with which he has survived, in the midst of circumstances which have caused the extermination of many of his early ancestors. Today the wild beasts of Africa are being

[23]

Adventures in the African Jungle

driven back mile after mile into the strongholds of forest, hill, and mountain; but wherever animal rights still triumph over human invasion, old Tembo remains the jungle's overlord.

EDITOR'S NOTE:

On October 18, 1924, Carl Akeley married as his second wife, Miss Mary L. Jobe, explorer, alpinist and educator. That same year the Canadian Government named one of the highest glaciated peaks in the Canadian Rockies, Mt. Jobe, in recognition of her writings and explorations. The 1926 Akeley-Eastman-Pomeroy expedition was Mrs. Akeley's *first trip to Africa*.

CHAPTER II   MY LITTLE KIKUYU FRIEND

BY CARL AKELEY

BILL began life as a little Kikuyu 'pickaninny.' He was born in a tiny mud hut on the foothills of Mt. Kenya. Though possessing and requiring little personal equipment all during his early boyhood—Kikuyu children wear practically no clothing—Bill was by no means lacking in his mental endowment. From infancy he was keen as mustard and agile as a leopard. Few items of importance escaped his quick eyes and his accurate little brain. If ever there was a child of destiny born into the world, Bill was that one.

Bill's father was very old and he was accordingly very wise. Bill had several half brothers and sisters—much older than himself—and they may have helped in his early training. But the first ten years of his life were spent in his father's *shamba* (field)—one of hundreds on the great, broad base of one of Africa's mighty peaks. During the long, warm days he played or worked in the fields of sweet potatoes, yams, *mealies* (corn), squash and beans. There, he drove his father's cattle, sheep and goats to a large spring of sweet water—the richest treasure Bill's father owned—that they might drink their fill. And there, too, after the sun had set and the swift twilight signaled the dark and early night, Bill squatted close beside the *shamba* fire watching his mother boiling corn and savory mutton stew of Kikuyu fat-tailed sheep.

Scattered out over the other hills were tiny points of red flame where other hungry little 'Kukes' watched the boiling pots. Great clouds of sweet wood smoke hung between earth and sky. Strong, chill winds blew off the icy summit of the majestic mountain. Bill wrapped his scant goat skin tightly around his sinewy little body and hugged the glowing fire. Way up in the density of the dark forest elephants trumpeted. Bill knew exactly what they were doing, because once in the late afternoon the chief of the Kikuyus, 'Ndagua, had taken him up on his high hill where they had watched the great herd until the twilight fell. They had gazed at the little ones at their play out in the open, rolling about a gigantic football—the hard clay of an old ant hill. They had watched them, alarmed by some passing wood cutters, return to the big herd. They had seen, but not heard, the great beasts swing silently through the forest. They had later listened to their trumpeting—calling the alarm to any stragglers—massing themselves against any danger.

Bill had felt the thrill of something new and terrific that day 'Ndagua had shown him his first elephants. Now he felt it all again as he crouched over the cheering embers and listened to the distant call of the great beasts. Again the thrill of the wild played all through his sensitive little soul and he began to dream of the days when he with some great *Bwana* (master) would hunt elephants in the vast and beautiful forest that clothes the gigantic ramparts of Mt. Kenya.

* * * * *

The boy was probably twelve or thirteen years of age when he attached himself to my *safari*. For a day or so he had been staying about camp always finding something to do. His great black eyes were ever on the alert. He jumped at the slightest chance to make himself useful. His slender, almost fragile hands were ever helping cook and tent boy, quickly passing them the things they needed in their tasks. The naked little shaver was in search of his *Bwana*—the hope of every smart native boy.

I decided to give the boy a steady job. His real name was Uimbia Gikungu but I immediately abbreviated this long native name to 'Bill.' A busy man cannot take time to pronounce six syllables every time he calls a black boy. He was made *toto* (helper) to the tent boy, Ali, and at once his training began.

In six months Bill had attained the rank of full-fledged tent boy, with plenty of leisure on his hands to have a try at almost everything else going on in camp. I think of him now, after four expeditions in which he has been with me, as the best tent boy, the best gun bearer, the best tracker and the best headman it has ever been my lot to know; a man who, I know, would go into practically certain death to serve me. If I were starting out on an expedition among unknown people in Africa, I would rather have Bill as a headman and as a counselor in dealing with the savages than any one I know of, even though they were people of whom he knew nothing.

During that first six months of his training in my camp, Bill was never idle. When there was nothing to do about the tents, he would borrow some traps and set them for jackals, or he would scour the bush all around camp in search of snakes and lizards which might be needed for the collection.

So the months passed. Bill, though always busy, remained an inconspicuous member of the *safari*. My camp was on top of the Aberdares, a mountain range west of Mt. Kenya. Cunninghame, the great elephant hunter, and I were returning from a fruitless four days' hunt. As we approached within a few hundred yards of camp, we crossed a fresh elephant trail. There ahead of us was one of our party with the tent boy, Ali, as gun bearer, hoping for a shot as the elephant crossed. A little farther on toward camp was Bill. The youngster was stripped to his waist and was struggling along with my 8 mm. rifle and a pocket full of 6 mm. cartridges. Bill had to be in on the game. It was thus that he showed his first interest in becoming the expert tracker and gun boy he now is—I believe without a peer in all Equatorial Africa.

Not long afterward, my work took me up into the Kikuyu hills, near Bill's *shamba.* He sent for his mother, to whom he wanted to give some of his earnings. When his mother came into camp, Bill introduced her. He led me out to where she stood leaning against a rock, and pointing to her said, 'Mama.' She was a sprightly young woman of the usual *shenzie* (low class native) type, dressed in a leather skirt, with hoops of bead-strung brass on neck and legs and arms, and with ornaments filling the large holes in her ear lobes. She was much younger than the stately old father whose second wife she was.

One day Bill was sulky and was scolded for not doing something he had been told to do. He said he knew his job and did not need to be told eternally what to do. He became irritated and often furious when he was ordered continually to do things which he knew to be a part of his routine. Never would he shirk his tasks. If he neglected to do his work at the proper time, in nine cases out of ten it was because someone had been nagging at him to do what he understood perfectly to be his job and it had the further effect of making him ugly.

At twenty this characteristic was as pronounced as it had been at fourteen. It has often been the source of serious trouble for Bill. Repeated orders implied for him a lack of confidence, and he wanted his good faith to be taken for granted, as does any serious, honest man.

When at last this expedition was finished, we returned to Nairobi to prepare for the departure to America. As soon as we reached the town, Bill demanded his pay. He was asked to stay until we were ready to leave Nairobi, but Bill, eager to be free to spend his earnings, left us, in spite of the fact that in doing so he sacrificed his *backsheesh* (gratuities). He promptly spent all his money for new khaki *safari* clothes, patterned after those worn by the white man. These he had made to order by one of the Indian tailors in the bazaar, and within two weeks he had lost all his new clothes in gambling. Thus ended Bill's first experience as tent boy on my *safari*.

Four years later, I returned to British East Africa. Several months before I arrived, Ali and Bill had been signed on for the Roosevelt expedition. But before I reached Nairobi, Bill had disgraced himself in some way, and had been turned out and black-listed. This censure meant that it would be very difficult for the

BILL WAS BORN ON THE FOOT HILLS OF MT. KENYA—THAT
GLACIATED PEAK ON THE EQUATOR.

Photo. by Carl Akeley.

BILL, WHO SAVED MR. AKELEY'S LIFE, IN THE KENYA FOREST.

boy to get another job. But knowing Bill's 'temperament' and the probable conditions contributing to his downfall, I was glad to take him on my safari, and Bill was glad to come to me again.

There were four in my party—and most of the other tent boys and kitchen staff were Swahilis—so we rather expected that Bill would have trouble, because there is little love between Swahilis and Kikuyus. But Bill's first real difficulty came as the result of an exaggerated sense of loyalty to me, or at least that was his excuse. During my absence from camp, one of my companions asked Bill for some supplies from a box to which Bill had the keys; but he refused to get them, saying that he must have an order from his own *Bwana*. It was cheek, and he had to be punished. The punishment was not severe, but, coming from me, it went hard with him, and I had to give him a fatherly talk to prevent him from running away.

Whenever we reached a government *boma* (post) or a town, we expected Bill to have a grouch. The bazaar thrilled him and tempted him to extravagance, just as it does all native boys. His strong impulse to spend his earnings and his keen desire to keep his money, too, put him in a dreadful state. On reaching Nairobi one thing almost invariably happened to Bill—he had to be paid in full and discharged. But once his orgy of spending was over, he would turn up the next day and would do his regular work with the greatest care but with a sad and gloomy face. Finally he would screw up his courage and say: "*Bwana*, will you take me on the next trip?" Then, when I had assured him that he could have his old job, his face would shine again and all his troubles would be over.

I now began to take him with me as an extra gun bearer when hunting dangerous game. Usually on such occasions he displayed a marvelous keenness of eye and ability to track. Soon he supplanted the regular gun bearer who perforce would have to bring up the rear.

One time, while hunting elephant in Uganda, I let Bill go with me. We had just finished inspecting a small herd. I had decided there was nothing in it I wanted, and had started back to take up the trail of another band. They were located in a section where the country was all trodden down by the spoor of two big bulls, and I told Bill to follow it, not thinking for a moment he would be able to hold it in the maze of elephant tracks. When last in town, the youth had bought a stiff brim straw hat and a cane, and he looked like anything but an elephant tracker, as he walked jauntily along, with his straw hat on the back of his head and swinging his cane like a dandy out for a morning stroll. For five hours the black boy followed that trail with the utmost ease, in many places where it would have given the professional tracker the greatest trouble,

Adventures in the African Jungle

and where nine out of ten would have lost it completely. At last it led us through dense bush. Bill suddenly stopped and held up his cane as a signal for caution. As I drew up to him, there were the two old bulls not twenty feet from us. When one of them was dead and the other gone, I felt much more comfortable than when I first realized the situation into which we had blundered.

But the time Bill earned my everlasting gratitude was when I was smashed up by the elephant on Mt. Kenya. Bill had been eager to go with me on the trip, but he had picked up a lot of English and was particularly desired by one of my companions, who spoke no Swahili, in order to assist in certain camp duties such as acting as interpreter in purchasing camp supplies from the natives. So somewhat regretfully, I confess, I had left him behind.

Bill was at the base camp when the news of my mishap reached it at dusk. It was past midnight before the relief party was ready to start to my assistance. Forest and jungle were enveloped in the blackness of a drenching rain. The *neapara* (headman) and the *askaris* (soldiers) were helpless, stupidly sharing the fear and dread of the forest at night which equally paralyzed the porters and guides. It was Bill—now completely master of the situation—who with a big stick put them all in motion. He crawled into their huts and compelled them to get out into line. Then, all through the remainder of the

[33]

Adventures in the African Jungle

dark night, he literally drove and herded them ahead of the rescue party, up the mountain side to me. And finally it was he who directed the cutting of the trail out of the forest for the passage of my stretcher, enlisting the services of a Kikuyu chief with his tribesmen, to chop a roadway from the *shambas* to meet my porters who were working downward. In this case, as in all other emergencies, Bill proved his mettle, his resourcefulness and his unusual intelligence—in fact it was Bill who without question saved my life.

While I was convalescing from the elephant smash-up, Bill was constantly on the alert for my welfare, assuming many of the responsibilities of the camp. Once he called on a porter to perform some service about my tent. The porter refused. Bill went out to 'interview' him. The porter was twice the size of Bill. There was a little scuffle and then Bill came in and did the job himself. Then he went over to the tent of the doctor who had been caring for me and took him out to where the porter lay. It required half an hour of the doctor's time to bring the porter back to consciousness. After this the other porters gathered about in a body, saying that Bill must go or they would all quit. I told them that the first boy who complained of Bill or refused to take orders from him would get 'twenty-five' (lashes). The average native would have taken advantage of the situation created by such complete victories—but not so with Bill.

Adventures in the African Jungle

He kept his dignity completely. Thereafter whenever he had occasion to give an order to a porter he always did it through the headman.

During this same period of convalescence, Bill's character was again admirably demonstrated. Although I was at this time able to walk about, I had to have someone accompany me and carry a chair, so that I could sit down and rest. It was now that an interesting event occurred in which Bill again had an active part.

At the edge of the Kenya forest, and only a short distance from camp, there was a great swampy area enclosed on three sides by a high ridge and on the fourth side by the dense, dark forest itself. One day the natives came into camp reporting that an old bull elephant had come out into this swampy place. They said he would probably stay in there for 'many suns.' It is customary for such lone bulls to appropriate one of these feeding grounds where they are not likely to be disturbed by their companions, and sometimes for a week or ten days to loaf around and feed and then vanish into the forest.

One morning Bill and I started out to look up this lone bull. We went to the edge of the forest where the natives showed us his trail. We followed it and found it joined by the fresh trail of a second elephant. I started to walk down the trail, but found I was not in physical condition to go on. So I sent the natives up and around the ridge bordering this crater-like opening. I told them

[35]

to throw stones into the bush as they went along. They had gone only a little way when one of the elephants was beaten out. He started to go across the bottom of the swampy depression right over open ground. He was probably three hundred yards from me and, as he approached the forest on the other side, it occurred to me that I might get him 'rattled' by shooting into the trees ahead of him. So I shot. The bullets crashed through the trees in front of him and frightened him. He wheeled around and started back. I had hoped he would come my way, but he did not. In the intense excitement, I shot at him three or four times. A little puff of dust from his dry hide told me the story of my aim and, while one or two of the bullets apparently struck in the right place, it was obvious there was not sufficient penetration to get results.

The whole affair was very foolish, but since I had wounded the beast, it was absolutely essential that I finish the job. The elephant turned again and went on across to the opposite side, and now I had to get on the trail and follow him. From a hundred yards away he got our wind and threatened momentarily to charge. Another shot turned him, and he disappeared into the bush.

An hour later I had a good view of the elephant at about seventy-five yards. It was under conditions where normally I could easily have gained a point from which I might have dropped him in his tracks. But now I was so exhausted that I took a shot at him from where I stood—seventy-five yards away. He went down, but got to his feet again and went into the bush. The black boys helped me back into camp. Although I felt certain we would find him dead in the morning, I knew the whole thing had been stupid and unsportsmanlike.

The next morning with a few of our boys I went back and took up his trail but, much to my disappointment and surprise, I found that the elephant and his companions had kept right on into the dense forest and were apparently going strong. I knew he was mortally wounded, and it was imperative that he should be followed up and finished off. It was too big a job for me in my convalescent condition. It was actually up to Bill. I gave Bill one of my gun bearers and each of them a heavy .470 cordite rifle with instructions to stick to the trail until they found the elephant. They were not to shoot, except in emergency. When the elephant was found, one was to remain with the animal while the other came back to report to me.

I returned to camp and waited. The boys had taken no food with them. I supposed they would show up before night, but it was not until midnight of the second day that Bill came to my tent and awakened me. He told his story of how they had followed the elephant without ever coming up to him—only once had they even heard him ahead of them—and of how they had finally deter-

Adventures in the African Jungle

mined it was best to come back to me for food and for instructions. Bill was almost 'all in.' The gun bearer, a big husky fellow, had collapsed entirely, and had been left on the trail some five miles back in the forest. Bill, ever faithful to his master's interest, had considered my elephant gun of more importance than our black gun boy, and so he had lugged both heavy guns back to camp. Fearing something might happen to the rifles, he had not hesitated to leave the gun boy alone in the forest with nothing but his knife for protection.

I realized, however, that the native would probably suffer no hardship except cold, and I knew without a doubt that he would build himself a fire. I could think of nothing to do until daylight. However, a half hour later an unusual noise in camp caused me to send for the headman. Bill came instead.

"What's the matter, Bill?"

"Boys won't go with me, *Bwana*. Every boy want to sleep. Never want to waken up. Never want to go."

"Go where?"

"Back to that gun boy with food."

Then I really woke up.

"Bring in the headman and the *askaris*," I commanded. "Now, tell them where to find the gun boy." Bill gave them full and definite directions. Then I ordered them to the boy's relief and my faithful Kikuyu to bed. This he finally did, after using up all his remain-

[38]

Photo. by Carl Akeley.

ENDAGUA, CHIEF OF THE KIKUYUS, SHOWED BILL
HIS FIRST ELEPHANTS.

Photo. Courtesy American Museum of Natural History.

MR. AKELEY BARELY ESCAPED DEATH AFTER BEING PINNED
TO EARTH BY AN INFURIATED ELEPHANT.

ing energy in protesting. The elephant was not found.

A year and a half later, when I had returned to America, Bill went back into the Kikuyu country and there began his search for the wounded elephant. He was clever indeed about the job. He not only discovered the native who had finally located the dead elephant, but he also found out all about him. The native had secured the tusks and had sold one of them to an Indian trader, but the second tusk he was still holding. Had the native observed the law in such cases, he would have turned both tusks over to the government officials. They would have paid him a nominal price for the ivory and I, having filed a claim with the government, would eventually have come into possession of the tusks. But the native must have reasoned that he would take a chance at selling them one at a time in order to get more money. However, he had made the blunder of leaving Bill out of the picture. Bill trailed down the case like a regular sleuth-hound, with the final result that the second tusk was sent to me and that the government confiscated a number of cattle belonging to the native, as penalty for his unlawful selling of the tusk. Thus, to both Bill and to me, the final outcome of that particular elephant hunt was satisfactory.

One time, in Uganda, I was using Bill as gun boy, in preference to the regular gun boy, because I had by this time realized that Bill was the best tracker, as well as the most keen and alert hunter—black or white—I had ever known. We had followed a small band of elephant into dense forest. For a long time we had been crouching in some undergrowth where we could occasionally glimpse the elephants' legs but nothing more. The elephants had been feeding quietly during this time, but at last they moved away and crossed a trail, down which we had a good view of them at a hundred yards. We thought the last one had passed. We moved quickly and quietly down this trail to the point where they had crossed. There we stopped, listening intently in the attempt to locate them. At first I thought they had gone out of hearing. Then I suddenly saw the rear elevation of a bull not more than twenty feet from us. He was motionless. We had come in so quietly he had not heard us. Now, I did not dare move for fear he would hear me. I craned my neck in an effort to see his tusks and, in so doing, I became aware of a cow elephant standing beside the bull, looking straight at us. Bill was five feet back and to one side of me. I stood motionless, without swinging my gun in the cow's direction. I was waiting for her to make the move—I doubt whether she saw us distinctly.

The bull now began to move away and the cow, turning to follow him, advanced a pace more or less in my direction. I was certain she would follow the bull, but to the boy there was no indication that I had even seen the cow. He thought she was coming at me. He raised his gun and fired pointblank into the cow's face. The elephant bolted. I wheeled and slapped Bill, because he had broken one of the rules of the game—the rule that a black boy must never shoot without orders, unless his master is down and at the mercy of the beast. Of course, I realized in an instant that the boy had shot in good faith, because he believed I had not seen the cow. He also believed she was coming straight at me. Poor Bill's heart was broken. I apologized as promptly and as humbly as the dignity of a white man permits.

The next day, Bill came to me, saying he wanted to quit—to go back to Nairobi. I made sure it was not his punishment of the day before that had brought him to this decision. He told me he was frightened and tired. He said the pace was too hot for him. The lad was having a case of nerves—in fact he seemed worn out. I persuaded him to stay, telling him he need not go with me for elephant for another week. I would take the other boys, and he could remain in camp. But the next morning, when I was preparing to go on the trail again Bill was on the job and refused to be left behind. He was later reported as having remarked that he "was not afraid for himself, but was afraid for his *Bwana*." We continued our elephant work at an easier pace than before.

Coming, as he does, from a gentle, agricultural people—among whom there are few hunters or gun bearers

Adventures in the African Jungle

—Bill has always seemed to me an exceptional individual. If it were not for the two occasions which I have related, I would say he is the only human being I have never seen tired out. He was ever insistently on his job.

Bill never was and never will be completely tamed. His loyalty to the master in whom he believes, and for whom he has an affection, is unbounded, and I firmly believe that the boy would go into certain death for such a master. He has a free spirit of independence which frequently gets him into trouble. He cannot bear to take orders from another black man. The Somalis and Swahilis associated with Bill on my *safaris* were constantly complaining to me, with the intention of getting him on bad terms with the master. From the standpoint of these two peoples, Bill came of an inferior race—the Kikuyus. Bill's disgrace with the Roosevelt expedition was due wholly, as I believe, to the Swahilis and Somalis who plotted against him.

When we had finished our lion-spearing expedition on the Uasin Gishu Plateau, many things had been stolen and the Somalis declared that Bill was guilty. A white man whom I had employed to take charge of the native Nandi spearmen disliked Bill. One day he ordered him to open his dunnage for inspection. Bill refused. When the case was brought to me and I investigated it Bill was so rebellious that it was necessary to punish him mildly. He ran from camp and I sent an

[42]

askari after him. The *askari* overtook him, but he did not bring him back because Bill had a long knife and he was prepared to use it to a finish. I then realized that I would have to see it through although my sympathies were all with Bill. Being near a government *boma*, I turned my case over to the officials. Bill was arrested, put in jail, and I went on without him.

Some weeks later, while making the ascent of Mt. Kenya back in Bill's old country, I realized more than ever how invaluable his services had been to me. I continually felt the need of my little native friend, and frequently I actually longed to have him back. I was up about ten thousand feet on the great mountain following an elephant trail. I had stopped to look at an elephant pit in which some animal had been trapped and from which he had made his escape. I was busy reading the very simple story. A giant hog had fallen into the pit and had worked with his tusks and feet at the sides of his prison, until he had elevated the bottom to a point from which he had scrambled out. All morning I had been wishing for Bill, because of certain troubles that were spreading among the black boys. Just as I was about to leave the pit and continue the march up the mountain side, I heard a voice behind me:

"*Jambo, Bwana.*" ("Good morning, Master.")

It was Bill's voice. I turned. There stood the most disreputable boy I had ever seen. His clothing hung in tatters and his shoes had almost reached the vanishing point. The only perfect thing about him was his grin. That was 'right as rain.' I wanted to hug him. I never learned just what had happened to the little fellow at the government post. I only knew that after two weeks he had gotten out and had followed our long and winding trail to the elephant pit in the gloomy bamboo forest of Kenya. He had probably traveled two hundred miles!

Bill remained almost my constant companion to the end of my 1912 *safari*. Invariably he showed his loyalty —his deep interest in all that pertained to my work and to my personal well-being. One time, we had been on an elephant trail a day and a half. I lay beneath a tree 'all in' with spirillum fever. I knew I could go no farther that day, so I ordered Bill to make camp. I was awakened from a light doze by the boy and when I asked him if my tent was ready he replied, "Your tent is not ready, *Bwana*, but your hammock is."

He had improvised a hammock out of two poles and a strip of canvas. He ordered me to get into it. He had redistributed the head loads, so that four of the strongest porters were free to carry me: then he made these black boys trot the ten miles to my camp. It was nearly a month before I had recovered sufficiently for us to take up the elephant trails again.

Another time I was down with black-water fever in

the Nairobi Hospital. I had been booked 'to go over the Divide' the night before, but, somehow, I had missed connections. When I regained consciousness in the tiny, hot and stuffy room, I opened my eyes with my face to a window looking out on a narrow back porch. There, looking over the rail at me, was my little Kikuyu friend, as watchful and faithful as any dog. It seemed to me that he remained standing there for hours, with tears in his eyes, staring at me. A few days later he was allowed to come into my room. He approached the foot of the bed, his small torn hat tight under his arm. I said, "It is all right now, Bill. I'll soon be well." With a murmured *"Jambo, Bwana,"* followed by a great gulping sob, he burst into tears and fled from the room.

Almost ten years after I left Bill in 1912, one of my friends, who had just returned from British East Africa, said to me at an African Big Game Dinner in New York:

"I know all about you now, Akeley. I have had Bill on my *safari* and he has never lost an opportunity to tell me stories about his *'Bwana Akeley'.*"

So I know that Bill is still loyal, and there is no one in all Africa whom I shall always be more eager to see. I missed him constantly on my trip into the gorilla country in 1921. If I had it to do over again, Bill would have met me in Cape Town. From the Cape to the Equator he would have lightened every burden for me. Not only in the arduous hunt for gorilla, when for the most part I was alone in the dense forests of the Kivu, but also in dealing with a strange native *safari* of Congo boys, Bill's services would have been invaluable. As I was unaided in the heavy taxidermic job of caring for the gorilla skins and skeletons, his help would have been without price, because, with his great aptitude for learning a new task or art easily and with his innate thoroughness, the boy had developed into a first rate taxidermic assistant.

Bill is nearly fifteen years older now than when I last said good-by to him as a lad at the end of 1912. He has attained man's full estate. He has been for many years in the service of some of the best of the African white hunters and has journeyed far and wide. I am confident that he has continued to be a valuable gun boy increasingly keen and efficient.

I hear he has his own *shamba*, a wife and three babies, that among the Kikuyus he stands as a man apart. And now, as I write this, with my next expedition (1926) in immediate prospect—an expedition which will be the most important of all my African undertakings—there is no one I shall be happier to meet than Bill once I get back to the land and to the work I love. I know how much in full confidence of faith I can expect from him, because I know the steadfast quality of his mind and heart—a quality which in Bill, the Man, can never change.

CHAPTER III   GIRAFFE

BY MARY L. JOBE AKELEY

THE most fantastic animal I have ever known is the giraffe. My first introduction to this extraordinary beast came just as our heavy train was puffing its way up the long grade westward from the Indian Ocean carrying us to the highlands of Kenya Colony. It was early morning. As I rubbed the red dust off my face and the sleep and cinders from my eyes, I gazed out of the window of our compartment, eager not to miss anything happening in this new land. Suddenly, out of nowhere in particular, three long, brownish-gray shadows moved right across my field of vision. For an instant only I glimpsed them and then the shadows faded as abruptly as they had come. I looked sharp in the direction whither the stalking creatures had vanished. Only a few straggling mimosa trees shimmered in the morning light. Perhaps I had only dreamed, over-anxious to see strange sights on this my first day in an unfamiliar land. Ten seconds passed, and the tropic sun shot swiftly up above the eastern rim. But out in the distant landscape which held my gaze, and right across a broad band of yellow light, three grotesque creatures stood out dark and definite in the brilliant sun. They were long of neck and long of leg and tail. They ambled slowly toward a shining stream. I had seen a vision it is true—but not the shadowy vision of a dream.

*   *   *   *   *

We were traveling down the long sloping hills from Meru to the Northern Eusso Nyiro. The sun, dipping low over the far-away blue mountains, reddened all the land. Trees and bushes, withered and brown in the dusty heat of noon, now glowed like burnished copper. Far down in the gray valley the twisting river had become a rope of gold. It was the hour of hours—the glorious finale of the day—before the swift-falling curtain of the tropic night.

I had stopped enchanted at the radiant beauty of the scene. All at once, a dozen rods away, a herd of giraffe appeared, twelve of them silhouetted against the brilliant sunset sky. Standing on a little rise of ground, they were beautiful indeed. Their tawny coats, crisscrossed with creamy white, shone resplendent in the roseate light. The giraffe were looking down into the valley. Then, becoming aware of our nearness, one after another, in quick succession they turned their long sinuous necks

[48]

and gazed intently at us with wondering eyes. Evidently they were curious but they showed no nervous fear. It was thus I had my first close-range view of this, to me, the most singular of quadrupeds.

I wonder how many of us have stopped to think how the giraffe got his name. It is derived from the word *'Zarafah,'* which is the Arabic name for the 'tallest of all mammals.' He is often spoken of as a *ruminant*, which means that he has a complex stomach and chews his cud like an ox. He is also referred to as an *ungulate*, that is, an animal with hoofs. In classic times the giraffe was called the 'camelopard.' This name was probably given when these animals were brought from North Africa to the Roman amphitheater where the Romans, always remarkably fond of exhibitions of strange and exotic beasts showed them at the time of their great arena spectacles and ceremonies. We can understand perhaps why the ancients arrived at such a name. The giraffe was another long-necked, long-legged animal with a rather awkward gait suggestive of the camel's, and with markings of creamy white and ruddy brown outstanding, just as in the coloring of the leopard's vivid coat. But certain it is, giraffe bear only slight resemblance in shape of body, and none at all in carriage, to the camel. In late Tertiary times, when the earth was overspread with great mammals of many kinds, giraffes ranged far and wide over southern Europe and India.

Adventures in the African Jungle

Today, however, they are found only in Africa, and there south of the Sahara.

For a month we lived right in the heart of giraffe country not far from the Equator. Our camp, pitched ten miles beyond the gleaming river, the Northern Eusso Nyiro, which we had first seen at sunset, was right in the midst of their feeding grounds. We were also near their water holes.

My husband wished to collect a group of giraffe for the African Hall of the American Museum of Natural History. As he needed one of the finest and largest old bulls, a splendid female and also a young giraffe, he began a careful study of the herds. Our task was by no means easy, because other *safaris* had recently passed through this region and all the animals had become unusually restless. In addition, the water holes soon began to dry up, and the giraffe wandered farther afield —on to the river to drink. These conditions greatly prolonged the time necessary for our work, but it gave us an unusual opportunity to become familiar with many of the habits and characteristics of the animal.

Every morning we arose long before the dawn, so that we could watch the giraffe while they fed undisturbed and before they began to move out of the sun's heat into the shade. They take their morning meal while all the vegetation is wet with dew, and it is surprising indeed to see how heavy the moisture often is,

Adventures in the African Jungle

even in this semi-desert country. After sunset the air becomes clear and crisp, and as the winds blow constantly from the great glaciers on the summit of Mt. Kenya, sixty miles away, the nights are so much cooler than the day that all the land is refreshed.

This northern, or *reticulated,* giraffe was not hard for us to locate, because his tawny, deep liver-red or dark brown coat is covered with a coarse network of white lines set in beautiful patterns. Before the sun is high, and when they are out in the open, they are spectacular indeed. It is only when they are partly obscured by trees, or stand in splotches of bright sun and dark shadow, that they are protected by their coloring. Of course, when out on the veldt, in the white light of noon, they become blurred and blended with the landscape, which is the case with all the other animals.

Sometimes a giraffe herd fed only a few rods from camp. Then we crept out quietly and watched them closely. I used to try to find two that resembled each other in the patterns of their coats, but invariably they were marked with different designs, not at all like the similar markings seen in domestic animals of the same family or breed. Often the herds came so near our camp that they could hear the cook's tattoo on his frying pan —the breakfast call. But they never stampeded at this sound nor at the general commotion and noise of the camp. Time and again we would see them stock still,

[51]

Adventures in the African Jungle

staring in our direction, just as if they wished we might tell them who we were and what we wanted. I was ever impressed by their steady gaze, their gentle inquisitive aspect, their apparent shy friendliness.

Sometimes we could go quite near to them, and they would nibble away at the thorn trees without even noticing us. And then, when we actually crowded on them, they would give ground slowly, often stopping in their tracks to watch us as we approached.

"If a man ever kills a giraffe, he never can forget the look in the dying animal's eyes," my husband once told me. "It is a look that will haunt you for weeks—a look of pathos and reproach."

It always seemed to me that the expression in their eyes was quite different from that of any other animal; that they wanted to tell us something or to learn something of us; that we were no doubt as amazing to them as they were fascinating to us.

One day we were photographing a big bull. We had secured the old male for the group and on this occasion were out only to make photographs. A solitary bull stood by the track our motors had made across the veldt. We photographed him at one hundred yards. Then we approached nearer and he continued to eat from the tree top. We moved slowly up to him and he walked even more slowly away, allowing us to gain a little on him. Then we finally photographed him at fifty paces. He posed for us, as we hoped he would, looking straight at us. It was an exceptional opportunity to study his every line and motion.

Another morning, fifteen giraffe, chiefly mothers and little ones, were out in the open a mile from camp. It was just before sunrise. The adults were not even grazing. They were standing quietly in a long line as if waiting for the warming sun, always grateful after the coolness of the night. Only the little ones frisked and jumped about, nibbling a leaf here and there and playing hide and seek among the grown-ups' legs. Two of the smallest were vigorously enjoying their breakfasts of mother's milk. We went close enough to them to get an excellent view of the herd and they did not stampede.

But when a herd of giraffe is disturbed, they move on in a most amusing fashion. Then they seem geared like a peculiar mechanical toy. They switch their long tails to and fro. Next the heavy black brush, which ordinarily almost touches the ground, is looped over their backs and off they go. They push through obstructing bushes while they stretch and bend their long graceful necks almost to the ground in order to avoid overhanging, horizontal branches. As they gallop, the 'near' legs and then the 'off' legs coördinate; that is, they move one side at a time. Their hind legs straddle out at each step and then advance one on each side in front of the fore legs. When you look at a giraffe from behind, he appears to move along without making any great effort whatsoever; but as you see him from the side his long neck swings back and forth as if on a big hinge. As he dashes off you wish with all your heart that he had been given a more dignified manner of locomotion. Unusual, stylish, almost regal in repose or at attention, he becomes ludicrous in his awkward gallop. However, he covers the ground at a great rate. It is said that only a very fat giraffe becomes winded quickly.

Remarkably enough, I have never seen the pace of an adult giraffe so swift but that the young ones could keep up without difficulty. The great naturalist and explorer, Samuel Baker, in recording his African experiences in the middle of the past century, wrote that the giraffe attained such a great pace because of the length of his stride and his bounding trot—that he is more than a match for any but a superior horse. He also declared that the giraffe's hoof is as beautifully proportioned as that of the smallest gazelle—his lengthy legs and short back giving him every advantage for speed and endurance. "There is a rule to be observed in hunting the giraffe on horseback," he concludes. "The instant he starts he must be pressed. It is the speed that tells upon him, and the spurs must be at work at the very commencement of the hunt and the horse pressed along at his best pace. It must be a race at top speed from the start, but should the

TIME AND AGAIN, THE GIRAFFE STOOD STOCK STILL STARING AT THE AKELEYS IN WONDERMENT.

giraffe be allowed the slightest advantage for the first five minutes the race will be against the horse."

When the herd gallops away it seems to move off with a single purpose as if its members were cavalry trained to respond to command. One or two may be on the alert —the rest feeding—but when they are alarmed and the stampede occurs, eighteen or twenty animals fall into close order and dash off as a perfect phalanx. A clatter of hoofs and a cloud of dust and the veldt is suddenly lifeless.

When I first saw the giraffe herds at a distance, the adults seemed to be almost uniform in size but after I had observed them for a while, I soon noticed striking differences. Often the mature females and the young bulls were quite matched in size, but when once the old bull leader of the herd came into sight it was a different story. He towered over the whole herd. Several of these old bulls were sixteen feet and more in height. My husband determined their stature by measuring the branches of the trees on which the animals fed. He used as a measuring instrument his gun barrel with a cord and weight attached. This device, plus his arm, totaled sixteen feet.

Often the long neck and legs of the giraffe make his body appear small and slender. But once a large animal is down, then and then only can you get a correct idea of

[55]

how large he actually is. It required half a day for my husband and his two assistants to skin the big bull for our collection; and it required an even longer time for five or six native skinners to remove the muscles from the great skeleton. Three days were spent by two men in 'thinning' the skin, that is, removing the extra tissue from the flesh side of the hide so that it could be properly cured and dried.

In the early days of the Kenya and Uganda Railway, the giraffe's long neck was always getting him into trouble. Here many a collision occurred between the animals and the telegraph wires. When the giraffe were traveling with head held low, to avoid the branches of trees and the thick bush, they were almost certain to run into the line which lay across their path. Then down came the wires and on went the giraffe. But the situation of the giraffe and the telegraph lines was no laughing matter in the late war. The animals were numerous in the region in which the English and Germans were fighting, in British and in German East Africa. It was indeed most serious to have the giraffe cut off field telephone and telegraph connections. There was only one solution —to kill off the giraffe. Tragic though it was to sacrifice these beautiful creatures, every giraffe found in the war zone had to be shot at sight. Thus the giraffe were practically exterminated in a large area of Africa.

As we watched the *totos* (young) they always seemed

Adventures in the African Jungle

to herd together. Some were so alike in size that they must have been twins. Two, and frequently four or five of these little ones, were regularly with one or two females. After observing giraffe over a long period of time, naturalists have stated as a fact that certain females act as 'nurse maids' to the *totos*. They watch them while they feed and as they romp and play, and finally round them up in time of danger or alarm.

In common with the rare okapi, giraffe have skin-covered horns. They are set close together and high on the head. Often there is a third horn, in advance of the pair and farther down on the forehead. The *totos* have quite noticeable tufts of bristly hair on the ends of their horns. These little adornments add greatly to the charm of their bright and jaunty little faces. Many a time in the top of a bush I would see something moving and there, peering out at us, was a baby giraffe, its eyes shining, its little horns abristle, its ears extended and its nostrils quivering. I always felt sorry that I could not go up to it and stroke its soft and lovely coat.

A decided advantage to the grown-ups is to be able to remain concealed behind the vegetation and to sight the enemy from over the tree tops. In a race with his greatest enemy, the lion, it is a question whether the speed of the giraffe usually permits him to escape. It must depend on whether or not the giraffe gets any handicap. When a lion springs from ambush, he is swift as an ar-

Adventures in the African Jungle

row and on the start he has a terrific get-away. But
although he can charge home with almost the velocity
and accuracy of lightning, yet he is quickly winded in a
long race. But a giraffe is said to have a powerful kicking and striking ability when in combat. The female my
husband obtained for his group bore the distinct scar of
a lion's claws extending the entire width of her gaudy
flank, from spine to belly. She, at least, had come off the
victor in a great contest with the King of Beasts.

The funniest sight of all was when the giraffe took
their morning drink. The herds used to come to a waterhole a mile beyond our camp and there from the shelter
of an old thorn blind near by we could easily watch them.
It was always an amusing show, chiefly because it seemed
to occasion the animal so much trouble to get his
nose down to the water. First he would approach cautiously, looking the landscape over all about him. Then,
very gingerly, he would step out into the 'hole' or
water pan. Next came a bending of his forelegs at the
knees. His feet were wide apart and his head was lowered
slowly. This action threw the whole body of the animal
so far back on his hind legs that he looked as though
about to 'squat' on his hind quarters. At last he was in position to drink, which he usually did for some time. Having slaked his thirst, he then began to 'pull himself together,' finally lurching into an upright position.

The Samburu natives, who were our neighbors in this

Adventures in the African Jungle

camp, told us that giraffe drink only once in three days. However, I have heard white men say that giraffe drink every day in the dry season when all the forage is parched, but less frequently when the leaves are soaked with rain and dew.

To watch a giraffe eat is almost as amusing as it is to watch him drink. His tongue is remarkable for its great length, often measuring seventeen inches in a lifeless animal. It has great elasticity and power of muscular contraction in the living animal, and it is covered with many large protuberances or *papillae*, as they are called. Like the trunk of an elephant, the tongue of the giraffe is an efficient organ for the examination and the grasping of food. It is truly remarkable to see him skilfully picking out the tender green leaves from among the thorns that are ever present on the bush or tree that supplies his food.

The giraffe is frequently supposed to be voiceless. A. Blayney Percival, twenty-two years Game Ranger of Kenya Colony, says that it was not until 1911, when he had had a good many years' experience with game in Africa, that he first heard a giraffe's voice. "I was sitting in a blind with my camera over a waterhole, giraffe and zebra before me, when I heard a curious cry; it was something like the bleating of a sheep, but infinitely softer. I am puzzled to express it in writing, but the syllables that most nearly represent it are *'wa ray'* rather prolonged. It was so soft that I could only just hear it at fifty yards. I was by no means sure that it *was* the voice of a giraffe, but it came so plainly from the direction of a cow that I watched her through my glasses and saw her mouth open to utter the call. I may add that I have never again heard a giraffe's voice."

Mr. A. L. Butler, Superintendent of the Soudan Game Reserves, has heard an old female in captivity utter 'a husky grunting sound' on one or two occasions when tantalized with food. Mr. Mostyn of the Egyptian Army has heard the same sound while photographing wild giraffe but he was unable to say whether it was made by a bull or by a cow giraffe.

Last spring while visiting my husband's old friend, Mr. S. A. Stephan, General Manager of the Cincinnati Zoological Park Association, he told me of an occasion in which he had heard the voice of a giraffe. I quote his own words:

"We have had three giraffe born here at the Cincinnati Zoo. The mother of the last one died when it was about seven months old. The mother was a very nervous animal, and whenever we had an electrical storm she would stand in the corner and tremble. As stated above, she died when the baby was seven months old, and by luck we got the baby to eat grain and other feed. The day after the mother died I came into the building and

[60]

heard a peculiar noise. I asked the keeper what it was and he said he did not know. I then walked up to the giraffe cage and found the noise was made by the little giraffe. It made a moaning noise just lifting one lip up whenever it made this sound. It missed its mother and worried a great deal, so I had the keeper stay in the cage during the day and pet it and feed it by hand. I heard this noise for three days only, and all of a sudden it stopped. You could hear it about 150 feet away. I am sure it is only the young giraffe that utter a sound. I have been in charge of giraffe for the past fifty years and have never heard a half grown or full grown giraffe make any sound whatever. The little giraffe died last Spring, and was nineteen years old when it died. The father of this young giraffe lived twenty-two years in our Zoo. The mother was about twelve years old when she died. These were the southern species of giraffe."

Fortunately, within the past few years, giraffe are widely protected in Africa and in such regions can be hunted only for scientific purposes. In some places, however, natives surreptitiously kill giraffe, shooting them with poisoned arrows and tracking the wounded beast until it dies a slow death. These natives are keen to secure the brush of the giraffe's tail, the long wire-like hairs of which they use as adornments for the arms and necks of their womenfolk. Many of them also eat the highly odorous flesh of the giraffe which usually contains considerable fat, and they use his heavy hide as sandals for their feet.

Almost immediately after we secured the big bull for our collection, dozens of the Samburu descended upon us, begging for *Twiga nyama* (giraffe meat). They had undoubtedly followed the vultures which had flocked to the kill and were perched by the hundreds on the trees near by waiting for their share of offal. These natives were willing to help skeletonize the huge beast, in fact to do anything whatsoever to assist in the great task, so long as we would give them the meat they craved. While the flesh was still warm with the animal's life blood, they heated or charred it a bit over a small smoky fire and then gulped it down ravenously in huge mouthfuls.

The odor of the beast was so strong that it required a great effort of will for me to remain near it while I prepared the lunch for my husband and his assistants. Bending unceasingly to their heavy task, in the blazing noonday sun, they got the full stench of the giraffe. I felt convinced that day that when you go to Africa on a collecting trip, it is well to leave your nose at home.

Some of our boys gorged on giraffe meat as enormously as did the native Samburu. The odor of its cooking permeated every nook of our camp. These black

THE AKELEYS APPROACHED CLOSE ENOUGH TO THIS GIRAFFE
TO SEE HIM WINK HIS EYES AND TO WATCH THE TICK BIRDS
ON HIS BACK.

Photo. by Carl Akeley.

TANGANYIKA TWINS—TWO BABY GIRAFFE, WHO
CAME NEAR THE AKELEYS' CAMP.

Photo. by Carl Akeley.

SOUTHERN GIRAFFE, MOTHER AND TOTO—WHOLLY
UNAFRAID OF THE AKELEYS' CAMERA.

boys held their feast long after our dinner hour. They squatted about the porters' fires, roasting their *twiga* on long sticks, while they sang and laughed and chatted as only natives with a good meal in store are wont to do; or they capered and danced about the flames, as if performing some mystic rite. The meat was so abundant, and their capacity so great, that even into the late night they continued to feast and make merry. As I went off to dreamland I could hear the sing-song of their minor chants and the soft murmur of their musical voices. Seldom do they laugh or speak harshly as white people do, and their melodious intoning blended like a lullaby in complete harmony with the witchery of the desert night.

The following day the boys began to dry the meat into *biltong* (jerked meat). A few of our boys, however, were strongly disgusted and said quite openly what they thought of anyone who would eat *twiga*. A great English hunter, however, has said that he considers 'fine fat giraffe splendid eating' and that 'it is difficult to imagine anything more tasty and succulent than a steak of young giraffe cow which is in good condition.' He regards giraffe fat a luxury after having lived for a long time on nothing but the dry meat of the smaller antelope. He says, however, that hunger, the sauce with which he had always eaten giraffe meat, might have

[63]

had something to do with his opinion. Some of the meat found its way to our table. To me its taste was just as unpalatable as its odor was unspeakable.

In marked contrast to the northern or reticulated giraffe is the southern or *tippelskirchi* giraffe. This animal is generally smaller and the pattern of his coat is blurred and indistinct. It is often called the leaf-patterned giraffe. The color-pattern of the body consists of dark irregular blotches on a yellowish fawn ground, quite unlike the network of creamy white on the reddish-brown ground which is the characteristic marking of his northern brother.

We found the southern giraffe numerous in Western Tanganyika and very easy to photograph. One day my husband experimented with our little camera car, attempting to see how close we could get to a single bull without stampeding him. It was clever and patient maneuvering, and he got results. We came within sixty feet of the giraffe. He stood calmly watching us. We could see him wink his eyes, could watch his nostrils quiver and distend while breathing. We used to go out in the early morning and watch the little ones take their breakfasts. Here we enjoyed the giraffe far more than in the north, because our hunting had been completed and we now had no interest in the giraffe save to watch and photograph them to our hearts' content.

Wherever we found giraffe we were sure to find their

red-beaked friends the tick birds. Long ago, in the hazy beginning of things the tick bird and giraffe made a compact that they would 'stick together' for their mutual benefit. The giraffe agreed to supply ticks to satisfy the appetite of his small friend and the bird promised to rid his long-necked ally of the leech-like pests. The plan worked well and today the descendants of the original partners may be seen carrying out their bargain. Riding fearlessly on the head, neck, body and even on the face of the giraffe, the tick bird gorges on the parasites while his host dozes or enjoys his own dinner from the tree tops.

All during our month's expedition on the Northern Frontier our boys, both personal servants and porters, had been wont to speak frequently and intimately of the old bull giraffe which had been secured for the collection. He had begun to assume a real personality as his skin had been thinned and softened, his skeleton cleaned and dried and all the bones numbered for identification and reassembling when later the construction of the clay model in the museum workshop would occur. After breaking camp it was necessary to drag and haul our motor lorries through the Northern Eusso Nyiro, too deep for them to negotiate under their own power. Every bundle, pack and load had to be portered across by the natives.

Now a great discussion soon began as to which black

boy should have the honor of portering the giraffe skin across the river. Cured, and thereby greatly lightened in bulk though it was, it still weighed a full hundred pounds. Now here is where the native is absurdly surprising. Often lazy and shirking in small matters, they were all eager to carry the old bull giraffe skin—the finest trophy of our hunt—over the ford. It was not an easy task. The water was waist deep in places and the boys knew that the 'crocs' were near by on their job of watchful waiting. And yet for days the palaver went on. Finally, the boys threw lots and the chance fell to the big Wanyamwezi, Kambi. Grinning all over his handsome face, he stepped up for the load. Certainly the giraffe must be the first to go across. He twisted up his big callous toes pointing to them and to the water and chuckling and whispering *Ngwena* (crocodile). Then, after two boys had helped him lift the load to his woolly head, he plunged into the river, chanting his "Hi-yi-yi, Hi-yi-yi" softly to himself in rhythm with his measured powerful stride. Without stop or hesitation, the precious burden rode high and safe and dry across the ford. And as Kambi reached the farther shore the watching natives and the white men, too, gave him the cheer he had earned.

Three hours later when our cars and all our paraphernalia had crossed the river we loaded our giraffe collection with great care and started on the four days' trail that led to our expedition base—Nairobi. And as we said good-by to the 'Gateway to the Northern Frontier'—to the region that had borne witness to success dearly bought, as all success is apt to be—my husband said to me: "Mary, when this whole expedition is finished, just you and I and Bill are going back to this wonder spot. It will be our holiday. We'll not have to shoot anything, but we shall spend a whole fortnight in watching and photographing and modeling and visiting with the Samburu natives and with their neighbors, the northern giraffe."

CHAPTER IV   IN SOMALILAND

BY CARL AKELEY

UNTIL comparatively recent years, little was known about British Somaliland. It remained an almost legendary East African country inhabited by primitive natives and fabulous beasts. There, according to rumor, dwelt the mythical unicorn. There, too, were to be found creatures that lived without water, if report was to be credited, and others that quenched their thirst with blood. In addition, tales were current of gazelles with giraffe-like necks and antelope no larger than fox terriers.

The chief reason for our expedition into this strange country was to obtain museum specimens of its rare and unusual animals before they were exterminated by ruthless hunters. Incidentally we were to seek whatever truth might be the basis for the stories concerning the incredible wild life of the land. On this latter point we were particularly successful, returning with proof of the existence of creatures so strange, so rare, and so

[68]

grotesque that the facts made fiction pale by comparison.

Somaliland was not new in the sense that it had never been visited or explored. However from its great numbers and species of animal inhabitants only a few specimens had ever been brought back for scientific study or for public exhibition. It was believed that our expedition might add greatly to the existing store of authentic information and that possibly we might make some discoveries of our own.

We found Somaliland a country where life was difficult for both man and beast. In many districts, water was extremely scarce and because of the hard, unfruitful character of the ground there was a minimum of edible vegetation. The grass-eating animals had to search continually for food and, in addition, they were beset by a host of foes. Existence was not much easier for the carnivora or flesh-eaters. However, despite hardships and handicaps we found game of all kinds plentiful.

There are three fairly distinct divisions in Somaliland so far as climate and topography are concerned. The coastal or maritime plain is a desert where the bones of men and beasts have whitened for ages under torrid suns. Approaching the interior, the land rises, becoming a plateau at an altitude of about 3,500 feet, where the air is dry and not uncomfortably hot. Beyond this partially forested tableland lies a second plateau much higher and generally arid and barren.

Adventures in the African Jungle

The natives of Somaliland withstanding the hardships of their unfriendly habitat are physically far inferior to many other African tribes. The animals with a few noteworthy exceptions—do not attain the proportions of their kindred in other parts of the continent.

In that parched country all living things have the ability to go a long time without water, and there are some creatures that have never been known to drink. Sometimes while marching tremendous distances—thirty-five and forty miles a day—even the natives exist for long periods practically without food or water. But their appetites are enormous and whenever food is abundant they will gorge themselves as if they never expected to eat another meal.

Although the Somali natives are divided into many different tribes, they are racially all about the same—a mixture of Arab and Negro. They are usually classified according to occupation or mode of life. There are four distinct native groups—the nomads, the town-dwellers, the traders, and the outcasts. The nomads lead a gypsy life, wandering from one end of the country to the other in search of forage for their herds of cattle, camels and ponies and for their flocks of sheep and goats. Year after year they follow the same route, visit the same camps and occupy the same rude shelters as they move on in their eternal quest for grass. The Somalis who live in cities are less numerous than the Nomads. They keep shops and engage in barter. The traders are seen only at intervals, as they spend most of their time far in the interior, where they obtain skins, ivory, horns, ostrich feathers, honey and coffee to be sold later in the bazaars. Last but not least interesting, are the outcasts, the Yebir, Tomal, and Midgan peoples. Living in scattered families, they are found throughout the land. The Tomals labor as blacksmiths, the Yebirs work in leather, and the Midgans hunt with poisoned arrows. All the outcasts are regarded as inferior by the dominant tribes, but their scorn is mixed with a trace of awe, for some of these 'social inferiors' are believed to be skilled in the practice of magic. More certain than the power of the black art, is the craft of the Midgans who with their terrible weapons seldom inflict a crippling wound but who quickly destroy their enemy.

The Somalis are generally good-tempered and friendly. I had one experience however which proves that this rule has exceptions. We had been hunting since dawn in a region of cruel heat and blinding sand. Thinking of nothing but the game we were pursuing, we failed to notice how quickly our water supply had diminished. In the middle of the afternoon we found to our alarm that it was entirely exhausted. We were many miles from camp, in a desert district where few white men could live more than twelve hours without water. Our situation would have seemed hopeless had not one of the natives told us he knew of a well not far distant.

Strengthened by the thought that we would be able to reach water within a short time, we struggled across miles of sizzling country until we came to the well. But the water hole was dry. Our hopes were shattered, and physically weakened by the additional march, our chances seemed poor indeed. The black boys now volunteered to look for another water hole, and we watched them set out through a stinging sand storm with a feeling that they were fated to fail. After an endless interval they returned empty handed.

There was nothing to do but await the end. I was too weary even to think. Then, suddenly I saw a caravan approaching. It seemed too good to be true. The advancing men were carrying heavy goatskins slung from the shoulders, and that could mean but one thing—milk! Quickly our boys ran out to meet them with offers to purchase the liquid that would save our lives. Even more quickly they returned, distress in every line of their features. The Somali caravan leader had refused to sell any milk. He would not part with even a small portion of his abundant supply. He was coldly indifferent to the fact that he was denying us life itself.

Equally heedless both to argument and to our proffered gold, the old villain started to lead his caravan away. I was utterly exhausted, but I was not willing to die while there still remained a single hope. Shouting to my companion to do likewise, I raised my gun and took deliberate aim at the nearest man in the retreating party. I would have fired without compunction, but before my finger pressed the trigger our self-appointed foes saw my raised rifle and surrendered. Their attitude changed in an instant. Whereas they had been content to leave us to perish, they now suddenly became willing —even eager—to satisfy our thirst. The milk was sour and had been carried in a filthy skin bag for hours under a hot sun but it was probably the best drink I have ever had in all my life.

In contrast to this unpleasant incident, there were many times when we received striking evidence of the natives' friendliness. When we were leaving Somaliland, the old chief, Dualla, who for months had shown me his devotion, now not only walked two hundred miles to say good-by, but he also crossed the Gulf of Aden in a small boat so that he might be with me when my ship sailed. As a parting present, he gave me one of his most cherished possessions, a string of Mohammedan prayer beads, of ebony, oddly and beautifully carved by his own hands.

It was really a very sad day for me when I learned of the outcome of Dualla's return trip. He never reached his native land. Homeward bound across the gulf, his frail boat capsized in a stormy sea. A few of his companions were finally picked up by a passing dhow, but before help arrived old Dualla had gone on the longest of all voyages.

All in all, in averaging the account of my experiences with the Somalis, I find that the credit side so overwhelmingly outweighs the debit that the latter seems small indeed. All of these natives are not heroic warriors. Some are lazy and others incapable of learning, but as a whole they are cheerful, reasonably intelligent and at times they display an amazing enthusiasm for their work. Perhaps they are not the most desirable companions of the trail, but they possess qualities which add something lasting and pleasant to a trip in their bitter and formidable land.

Many of our black friends took a keen interest in showing us the strange and extraordinary creatures of Somaliland. Sometimes they would make a special effort to bring to our attention some beast which they thought unusual and interesting. In fact, they were like farm boys showing city dwellers the 'sights' of their rural community.

One of our earliest acquaintances was the wart-hog. First encountered at Mandera, near the base of the Golis range, we continued to see this curious and hostile cousin of the pig nearly everywhere we went. If his beauty is impaired by the strange wart-like bumps on his nose and head, he is anything but laughable when he turns his murderous tusks toward the hunter in a charge.

Frequently the male has tusks more than ten inches long, and they are most unpleasant weapons considering the temper of the beast. He is a courageous animal, seldom giving any indication of fear. Perhaps his greatest enemy is the leopard. His favorite gait is a brisk trot and he presents quite a dashing figure when he moves through the bush, tail held upright and long mane abristle.

The natives who are Mohammedans never eat or touch the flesh of the hog. Any hunter who shoots one for food or for scientific purposes must be prepared to dress his kill and preserve the hide without the slightest aid from his servants, as they refuse to handle not only the animal but the skinning tools as well.

Another curious animal, with a domesticated relative, is the wild ass. They are handsome animals, with large heads and well-shaped bodies. In general their coat is blue-gray in color; but the nose and belly are white. This timid and rather friendly little fellow is rare. He is the only member of the horse family found in this part of Africa. I much prefer photographing animals to shooting them. However in order to obtain specimens for our museums it is necessary to do so. When the hunt involves a lion or an elephant, the danger to the hunter gives the contest a fairer aspect, but when it means shooting down such friendly and harmless animals as the wild ass, it is difficult not to feel like a murderer.

Although generally wary and quick to escape, we sometimes found the wild ass so tame that it was almost like going into a stable and shooting a favorite horse. Some of them lived in the barren district near the coast—some, in the mountains among the thorn forests. I doubt if there are many left today. They were never numerous and for years they have been eaten by both men and beasts.

We found many lions in the interior, thriving in a region so hostile that to hunt them often taxed our resources to the utmost. Compared to their brothers in other parts of the continent they are poor specimens. In no case did we find one with a fully-developed mane or with the truly leonine appearance. There was practically no water, and they undoubtedly drank the blood of their prey to save themselves from perishing of thirst. Without question, these poor fellows are responsible for the hair-raising tales about 'blood-drinking beasts.' With them, however, it was not a question of choice but of necessity.

The natives wage perpetual war against the lions, as the latter commit many crimes against native property, raiding the herds and flocks when their natural food the antelope is scarce. When a lion has carried off and eaten a number of sheep, goats, or young camels, from one particular settlement, its inhabitants organize a horseback drive. The Somalis and Midgans pursue their prey until, worn out by the chase, the lion stands at bay in the open. Then they surround him riding in circles— like the Indian warriors of our own western frontier days—while the victim wheels and turns, attempting to face each of his hundred foes. Soon he becomes confused and falls an easy victim to the poisoned arrows. Occasionally the lion sells his life at a high price, killing one or more of his assailants before the poison does its work. If he is enraged, the king of beasts can easily overtake a tired pony, and when that happens the rider will ride no more.

Greater even than the lion's destruction of cattle and sheep is the havoc wrought by the real 'gangster' of Somaliland, the leopard. He is the most dangerous of all the wild animals in that country. Compared to his brothers in more friendly regions, he is small, but he is vicious and will attack either man or animal. Only the camel seems immune from his slashing claws and wicked teeth. Although they will stampede at the first roar of a lion, these hump-backed beasts of burden stand at ease even when leopards crawl among them.

Once we saw the carcass of a hyena suspended from the fork of a tree fifteen feet above the ground. A leopard had placed it there. Such feats of tremendous strength and agility are by no means uncommon, for, despite his relatively small size, this big spotted cat is one of the

Adventures in the African Jungle

most formidable of the carnivora. Antelope, wart-hogs, sheep, goats and even children are included in the leopard's larder. Grisly remains of his feasts are frequently found near the dens in the cliffs where he makes his home. And if one hears a hoarse cough while inspecting such remains it is well to grab a gun or leave the neighborhood for you may be sure the leopard (*Felis Pardus*) is on the premises.

The leopard will frequently attack in circumstances where even a lion would retreat. Whereas the lion is always a gentleman, the leopard is little better than a thief with murderous tendencies. My personal experiences with this member of the cat family, in all parts of Africa where I have found him, have taught me that leopard hunting at its best is never a safe business for the hunter. In one encounter with the 'tabby' I was seriously lacerated from wrist to shoulder and I can testify to the razor-like sharpness of their wicked, disease-carrying teeth. This was one of the episodes of my visit to Somaliland, but the story of that long struggle must be told in a later book.

Of the many magnificent animals that make their homes in Somaliland, the greater koodoo is one of the most fascinating. It is among the largest of known antelopes, and the male of the species carries majestically a pair of long spiral horns among the finest trophies in all Africa. Beautifully colored and powerfully built, the

THE WART HOG IS A COURAGEOUS ANIMAL—FREQUENTLY HIS
TUSKS ARE MORE THAN TEN INCHES LONG.

Group collected and mounted by Carl Akeley.   Photo. Field Museum of Natural History.

THE RARE WILD ASS IS THE ONLY MEMBER OF THE HORSE
FAMILY FOUND IN SOMALILAND.

Adventures in the African Jungle

greater koodoo lives in the mountains, where his agility in climbing gives him an advantage he would not have on level ground.

When the male koodoo passes through wooded country, where low branches impede progress his horns are a hindrance. Probably this is why the koodoo is seldom seen except on high ground, where thick vegetation is scarce. The male has a long mane and beard, dark brown in color, the hair of the latter sometimes reaching nine inches in length. The female is hornless. It is she who is the sentinel for her lord and master. When alarmed, she gives a sharp, startling bark which immediately notifies all members of the herd of their danger.

As the Field Museum particularly desired a group of these animals, hunting the greater koodoo was one important part of my work in Somaliland. The old bull now in the museum, shown standing with lifted head and on a high rock was the second koodoo that I ever saw. He was on the run when I fired; the first bullet sent him leaping into the air and my second shot finished him. Strong, and possessed of an amazing agility for his weight, the greater koodoo frequently sets a pace across rough ground that will discourage the most enthusiastic hunter. And unless the first shots are effective, the animal will almost certainly be out of range before a rifle can be reloaded.

In connection with koodoo hunting I tried an experiment that seemed to work out, but it may have been only my good luck. I sighted an animal that seemed especially desirable for the group, but unfortunately he had seen me first, and before I was within a mile of his original stand he had completely disappeared. I tracked him until I lost his trail. Then I had an idea. I tried to think of what I would do if I were a koodoo pursued by an enemy. Looking around the country, I selected a route offering the most difficulties to the hunter, and I took it. Several times reason told me I was off the trail. Once a heavy spider web stopped me. If the koodoo had gone that way, the web would have been broken by his passage. I changed my direction a little and kept on. For several miles I followed this course, always taking the route which it seemed to me the animal would follow. At length I reached the top of a ridge which commanded a wide ravine. Crawling to the edge, I looked down, hoping to find my koodoo, but I could not see a sign of him. Disappointed and about ready to give up the hunt I stood out in the open hoping that if he were in the ravine he would be frightened at me and break cover. As I got to my feet I saw him about three hundred yards away running full speed in the opposite direction. A shot and the desired trophy was mine. My experiment had been successful. The results of that stalk and of several others now stand in the halls of the Field Museum in Chicago.

Adventures in the African Jungle

The lesser koodoo is an interesting relative of the greater koodoo, but he differs from the latter in many respects. Unquestionably a beautiful antelope, he is perhaps the handsomest of all those found in Somaliland. The lesser koodoo prefers the forests on the low ground at the base of the Golis to barren mountainous country. The head and neck are marked with white, and there are usually eleven to thirteen white stripes about the body. The ears are very large, and the male has spiral horns resembling those of his big cousin. There is a great difference in the coloring of the male and female. The bucks have blue heads and necks—sometimes an old one will be almost black—and the does and young ones are of a brownish color.

Usually about six lesser koodoos are seen together, but, whether observed individually or in a herd, they are always stylish and appealing. It is a pleasure to watch their movements when vaulting over bushes and other obstacles. They display the ease and grace of birds in flight. Once startled it is very unlikely that the hunter will get another view of the agile creatures who never pause when frightened until their flying hoofs have covered considerable distances. Because they are among the most wary of animals there are very few complete collections.

At the time of our visit, Somaliland was particularly rich in antelope life. Besides the koodoo, there were oryx,

Adventures in the African Jungle

Swayne's hartebeeste, Pelzelin's, Speke's, Spemmering's, Clarke's and Waller's gazelle, as well as dik-dik.

The oryx is the creature which the ancients considered a fabulous and fearsome beast. The ancestors of the present-day oryx served as models for the authors and illustrators of olden times when they used their imaginations to supplement natural history and created the unicorn. Viewed in profile, the oryx seems to have but a single horn set near his nose, and his sturdy, donkey-like body completes the parallel between him and his mythical predecessor.

The oryx is able to live for long periods without water. And the region he inhabits is one where wells and drinking holes are few and far between. Sometimes we saw as many as fifty of these animals in a single herd, but more often they were in groups of a dozen or less. In the waterless, treeless plains of Toyo and Silo, they were plentiful, grazing on the harsh dry grass, their long horns outlined against the sky. Since their horns are dangerous weapons, it is unsafe to approach within striking distance of a wounded oryx, because true to the unicorn tradition at such a time he will attack without hesitation.

The horns of the average oryx male in Somaliland are about two and a half feet long, but in this respect the female sometimes excels her mate. It is not unusual for her horns to attain a length of even three feet. I have

seen males fighting among themselves, thrusting and parrying like two human duelists engaged in sword play.

The natives, coveting the skin of the bull oryx for shields, frequently organize horseback hunts in order to run down their prey. These hunts are such savage affairs that at the conclusion it is not unusual to find one or more of the natives and their mounts impaled upon the rapier-like horns.

Oryx calves are amusing little fellows resembling somewhat the calves of domestic cattle. Their 'voice' is between a bleat and a bellow and they can run even faster than full grown members of the herd. Once we captured a little oryx calf and brought him into camp where he quickly became tame and friendly. He learned to suckle a goat, and it was laughable to watch him take his dinner, as the goat was less than half the size of her adopted baby.

On the elevated plateau south of the Golis range and north of Ogaden, we found the rare, ungraceful and timid Swayne's hartebeeste. Seen in herds ranging from half a dozen to many hundreds, they inhabit plains where the bushes are seldom over two feet high. It is difficult to approach them, as their eyes are keen; they persist in keeping a considerable distance between themselves and strangers; and they are clever in eluding pursuit. When disturbed or frightened they possess the tantalizing habit of moving only a short distance at a time, thus

Adventures in the African Jungle

permitting the hunter to come fairly close. Breaking into their clumsy-looking canter, they run a short distance, halt, look back and wait until the man gets dangerously near, when they repeat the performance. Both sexes possess horns, but I do not consider the hartebeeste a game animal, or particularly desirable as a trophy. Shooting them is a sport I dislike extremely. In an emergency their flesh may be used for food but it is too dry to be eaten with relish.

Somaliland was so rich in unusual animal life that our daily work sometimes brought unexpected discoveries. One day while looking for koodoo I had an experience which I shall never forget. In the distance I saw four animals on a rock-strewn hill beneath an acacia tree. Believing them to be koodoo, and as I needed two more specimens to complete my museum group, I advanced cautiously, attempting to get within rifle range. From the cover of a bush I had a good view, and I judged them to be about 200 yards away. I fired and one dropped in its tracks. The other was startled. However he had not located me and only ran about in a confused manner. My second shot dropped another, and a third bullet wounded one which ran almost directly toward me. He came so quickly that I was greatly surprised. I quickly concealed myself in a bush a short distance away. Then I began to realize what was happening. What I had thought were koodoo more than 200 yards distant were

in reality much smaller beasts less than 150 feet from where I stood. They proved to be pygmy antelope—a very rare species that had never before been recorded! I had been completely fooled, because there was nothing in the surrounding country of known size by which I could establish a scale.

I went into the bush where the wounded animal had fallen and stood for a moment gazing at it in wonder. Never had I seen such an antelope. It had sharp straight horns, about four inches in length and the body was a beautiful French gray in color. Standing, it would have been less than two feet high at the shoulder. Before I could observe anything more, it sprang to its feet and darted away on three legs, faster, it seemed to me, than anything I had ever seen travel on four. I fired several times but missed completely. And I followed for hours without overtaking it.

Later I learned that it was one of the little beira antelope. The species had been described some time before from fragments of skin obtained from natives but as far as records show, my specimens, an adult female and a half-grown one, were the first ever taken by a white man. The outline of the beira, with its large ears, is almost a miniature of that of the koodoo, and that, with the illusion of distance created by their small bodies, were the circumstances which led to my discovery. I continued hunting the beira in an effort to get a male and

thus complete the group. Several times, I spent the entire day working about two cone-shaped hills, now and then catching a glimpse of my quarry, only to have them disappear before I could shoot or get near enough to shoot. Frequently at dusk, before starting for camp, I would turn around to see on the skyline just the heads and necks of three little creatures watching me as I went away discouraged. Of all the antelope we hunted, they were the most difficult to obtain.

As chance entered largely into my beira hunt, so it did in many of my other adventures elsewhere. Another record came equally by good fortune. One evening when coming out of the forest, after some rather troublesome experiences with elephants, I caught sight of a bush buck. He saw me, too, and, instead of beating a retreat, he stood stamping his foot and seemingly glared at me. I may have imagined his emotions but it appeared that all the animals were angry with me that day. I remember the thought going through my mind, "I believe this fellow is going to charge too." Then I recalled that we needed meat in camp, so I shot him and told the boys to cut him up and bring him in. As soon as they reached the body, they shouted to me and I went to see what was the matter. They showed me an unusually fine head. I saved it and it turned out to be the record bush buck head of that time.

Another kind of pygmy antelope which we encoun-

tered frequently was the dik-dik. There are three varieties inhabiting Somaliland; Swayne's, Phillip's and Guenther's. Of the three species, Swayne's dik-dik is the smallest. I could distinguish this little fellow readily from the others by his different hued and lighter coat. Usually only the male and female appeared together— sometimes accompanied by a young one. The female always led the way, her mate following at a short distance. If a young one was present, it preceded both parents, its little pipe-stem legs moving with a rapidity too fast for the eye to follow.

Dik-dik seem unable to go for long periods without water, although we saw some of them in localities where it was difficult to procure. Frequently we met them feeding on leaves and shoots of bushes, but the instant they detected our presence they would go bounding away, like rabbits and at an astounding speed.

Phillip's dik-dik is not only larger but it is different in color, ranging from a rich reddish tinge to dark mahogany, the dark back and pure white belly presenting a strong contrast. When alarmed, the dik-dik utter a shrill whistle which is repeated two or three times before they stampede in a series of jumps which make them look as if they were mounted on springs. It is an amusing sight to see several of them leaping over low bushes and occasionally bounding high in the air as if to look back and gauge the distance between them and their pursuers. They are delightful little creatures, and their immense eyes give them an especially gentle appearance. This greatly enlarged eye, with its light hazel iris, is naturally associated with night-roving animals, but our friend the dik-dik seems to have no trouble in seeing clearly in the brightest daylight.

We first met the Guenther variety at Dagahbur, and found it together with the Phillip's throughout Ogaden. Its long muzzle and its greater size make it easy to distinguish from either Phillip's or Swayne's; but even without these characteristics it would be easy to differentiate it from the other dik-dik, as it lacks their beautiful, contrasting colors. Sometimes we saw as many as a dozen in a single band.

With the possible exception of the dik-dik, the one member of the antelope family we encountered most frequently was the gerenuk or Waller's gazelle. No matter how often you see this animal, it never fails to impress you with its peculiar appearance. Imagine an antelope that looks something like a young giraffe; think of it standing on its hind legs with its head appearing in the topmost branches of a bush; picture it walking with a careless slouch and running with its long neck dropped to a level with the body. If you can succeed in visualizing all these things, then you may have some idea of what an odd chap the gerenuk really is. Then add to this conception the fact that no one has ever seen him drink, and

Group collected and mounted by Carl Akeley.

Photo. Field Museum of Natural History.

WHEN THE DIBITAG RUNS IT CARRIES BOTH HEAD
AND TAIL WELL UP AND TRAVELS SWIFTLY.

GROUP OF GERENUK COLLECTED BY CARL AKELEY IN SOMALILAND.
THEY ARE STRANGE CREATURES WHICH HAVE NEVER BEEN SEEN TO
DRINK.

you will begin to understand why we found him such an interesting acquaintance.

The male stands about four and one-half feet high, a considerable portion of this height being due to his exceedingly long neck. By standing four and one-half feet high, I mean when he is on all fours; but at dinner, or at any other meal, the gerenuk is more than likely to have his front legs on the table, that is he stands on his hind legs while his front legs are in the shrubbery on which he is feeding. His whole body seems stretched to the utmost as he extends his head and neck in order to crop some dainty morsel.

He is not a graceful fellow in any posture, and, when his eyes peer out at you from the top of a thorn bush, it is hard not to laugh at him. However, if he sees you first, he literally fades into the parched vegetation. It is folly to look for him in the place where you have seen him last. Until we learned this we ran head on into many a thorn bush while the gerenuk ate his dinner elsewhere.

We met the gerenuk feeding on the leaves of the thorn tree and aromatic bushes growing in the driest regions. Even when water holes were abundantly filled, he seemed uninterested and it was indeed amazing to watch him browse at the tempting brink of a pool without once lowering his long neck to drink. Perhaps the gerenuk is a stupid animal. At all events he does not possess the wariness and ability common to all the other gazelles to take care of himself. Fortunately for the survival of the animal in Somaliland, the natives have a decided prejudice against eating its flesh.

In contrast to the graceless gerenuk, is the sprightly, handsome, and exceedingly wary Clarke's gazelle. It is a rare animal known to the natives as *dibitag*. On our expedition, when most kinds of game were plentiful, this animal was seldom seen, and it was always difficult to approach. Its neck is so slender, its head so small and pointed, and the purplish gray color of its coat matches so well the surrounding bushes, that it takes an expert eye to distinguish animal from landscape. The moment a dibitag starts to run, there is no mistaking it for any of its Somaliland companions because its movements are entirely different. Carrying both head and tail well up, it bounds away, clearing bushes with easy grace at every jump. We encountered it in the jungle of the umbrella mimosa and in the glades of *durr* grass.

Another gazelle, Speke's gazelle, we found on the high plateau. Pelzeln's, we saw in the lowlands, in a district so barren and dry that we wondered where and how it found sufficient nourishment to sustain life. Very seldom did I meet one among trees of any size, although occasionally I have seen them in bits of jungle, which they probably sought in order to elude pursuit. Although Speke's gazelle is a shy creature, he possesses considerable curiosity and will stare at a man for a long time before starting to run. When first startled, the animals will not go far. If not again molested they will soon begin to graze or play, the males engaging in sham battles and chasing one another with great bursts of speed.

Even so long ago as 1896—the time of our expedition—the aoul or Soemmering gazelle was in danger of being killed off. We then saw large herds south of the Golis range. Their extermination is almost certain because, being neither suspicious nor wild, they fall a quick and easy prey to the guns of ruthless hunters. From my own observation I would say that they can exist indefinitely without water. They live in a region which is almost as 'dry as a bone.' There are no rivers between the Shebeyleh and the sea. The natives obtain their supply of water by digging in the dried up beds of the *tugs* (streams), but the gazelle, unable to thus fend for himself, must depend on chance water holes left after the rains. Both the male and female aoul have horns, differing a foot or more in length.

The ugliest and certainly the most cowardly of all our Somaliland acquaintances was the spotted hyena. He is a filthy villain—vicious as any cut-throat. We met him everywhere, except in the wild ass country. In parts of Ogaden his breed was so numerous that they became an offense to me and a blemish to the landscape. As a rule they were covered with disgusting sores, probably caused

Adventures in the African Jungle

by the impure condition of their blood, since they live almost entirely on carrion. Their combats among themselves may also have had something to do with their disreputable appearance.

The hyena's voice is both powerful and hideous. When night and hunger brought them close to our camp we were treated to a concert of long-drawn-out wailing notes that did not add to our cheerfulness, and when they were excited they rendered another 'song' as an encore. Thinking it over, I am not sure but that the second variety was worse than the first. Their shrieking laugh always seemed to me like the terrifying cry of some poor tortured maniac.

As a scavenger, the hyena has some value, but his vices are such that by comparison this one virtue seems negligible. He does his best to save his loathsome body from all danger. He has a set of vicious teeth. His jaws are like a steel trap. Pity the wretch of a native whose sleeping place is invaded by this slinking terror, for with one frightful snap he will carry away the entire face of his human victim. The beast's appetite is seemingly without limit. It is only equaled by his wariness, which makes it difficult indeed for the natives to revenge themselves with their primitive weapons. Consequently the Somalis are happy when the white man's rifle takes heavy toll of the brutes.

Once I had an unpleasantly close contact with a hyena.

Adventures in the African Jungle

I was aroused from my sleep by a great commotion. My bed suddenly began to pitch and heave and in a moment I was tossed out on the ground cloth of my tent. A hot and filthy breath was in my face. I jumped quickly for my gun, just as a dozen natives rushed in and the beast rushed out. A babel of shrieks and human howls, and in a little while I was told what had happened. Probably following the scent of meat, a hyena had crept into camp and had prowled around until it came right upon the sleeping natives. It had seized one protruding black foot, and the native had been saved only by the prompt action of his comrades, a score of whom attacked the beast. Seeking escape, it had bolted wildly, dashing under my tent in its frantic effort to reach the freedom of the plains.

We did not see nearly as many striped hyenas as we did the spotted variety, although both were widely distributed throughout the country. There are two recognizable forms of the striped hyena, known to the natives as *dedar* and *werra*. The latter, our boys told us, is by far the more destructive, killing sheep and goats merely for the love of slaughter. It is smaller than the *dedar* and the stripes are more numerous and almost black. Both types of the striped hyena make a better appearance than do their spotted kinsmen. They are rather prepossessing, with their long fur and thick bushy hair.

At an impromptu Somaliland feast, the jackal sits at the lion's table but he keeps a respectful distance,

[93]

Adventures in the African Jungle

accepting whatever scraps the King of Beasts chooses to discard. We saw so many jackals that we came to know them well, and always found them without the disagreeable qualities of their evil associates. A jackal frequently amused us by trotting along just as carelessly as any dog in full view of our party. If someone whistled, he would stand for a long time looking at us, as if trying to determine what we were.

Keen of scent and constantly on the move, the jackal is a menace to the kids and lambs in the flocks of the natives, but he lacks strength to attack the larger animals single-handed. However, if there is any meat in the neighborhood, he will discover it and will be on its track immediately. He, too, has a voice that is often heard. Even now I can hear his long-drawn plaintive howl as he loitered about our camp in those distant days.

Looking back on our adventures in Somaliland, I think of it as a country more fascinating, more singular and even more alien than it appeared to me when first I stood upon its charmed shores. Its hardships and its dangers have almost faded from my mind, but the thrills of new sights and of continual and intimate contact with the strange wild folk of that stern and splendid land will ever remain as dear memories.

Unquestionably infinitely fewer animals live in that far away land today. Where there we saw great herds of game, a desert may now easily exist. It is doubtful

Photo. by Daniel G. Eliot.

CARL AKELEY IN SOMALILAND.

GROUP OF SPOTTED HYENA COLLECTED BY CARL AKELEY
IN SOMALILAND.

Adventures in the African Jungle

if an explorer in this day would find more than a remnant of that rich and abundant wild life which so delighted us. Our expedition was successful in obtaining specimens of nearly all the desired species, and these may now be seen, mounted in groups in the halls of the Field Museum in Chicago. That was the primary purpose of our trip. But, surely and definitely as our work was being brought to a satisfactory conclusion, there came to us, with the toil and stress, the real and the unforgettable joy of a constant association with the denizens of mountain and of plain. And now after more than thirty years I like to think back on those days when we were not compelled to fire a single shot but when we could devote all our time to the pleasure of photographing and studying the friendly, four-legged folk. I like to remember the animals undisturbed and untamed, living without fear or care of man, as wild and free and as beautiful as was the country which they had chosen for their home.

CHAPTER V   A NIGHT BY THE WATER HOLE

BY MARY L. JOBE AKELEY

THE King of Beasts shares one possession with his low-liest subject and with all the horned, hoofed, feathered and fur-bearing creatures of the land of perpetual summer. At some time during the day or night—and it is usually the night—the lion and all the other animals which walk in kindred ways must leave the secret places of bush and veldt to quench their thirst. They congregate at the water hole—the common meeting place, and there in consequence the story of the jungle is written plainly at its trampled edge.

Every water hole is a place of tremendous action and of swift drama. It is a scene of ambush and of murder. It is the rendezvous of friends, the battle ground of hereditary enemies—the one spot where the weak and the strong, the cowardly and the courageous come willingly to face their death in quest of life-sustaining water.

In Africa all life is dependent on the rains. From late

[96]

Adventures in the African Jungle

February until the end of May, when the rain gods usually smile, the earth receives its richest blessing. As the storms gather, the world takes on a different aspect. The skies are overcast; strong winds begin to blow; birds become noisy and active, and the natives gather to plant their crops in their clean dug *shambas*. Then the first downpour comes—by no means the soft and gentle April shower we know at home. Deluge, lightning, booming thunder, darkness in the day—all attend God's greatest gift to man. At last mountain brook, lake and river are replenished and all the land is made glad with copious flood and freshet. In an hour the dry stream bed becomes a rushing river, and when the flood recedes deep pockets in the clay catch and hold the remnants of the torrent. These natural reservoirs are the desert water holes, or water pans, where the animals find refreshment for many weeks to come.

No one who has ever seen the gathering and the breaking of the rains is likely to forget it. Stormy days—clean, sweet air—cool, fresh nights. It is the climax of the tropic year. Theodore Roosevelt was so tremendously impressed by the spectacle of equatorial storms that he described it in epic prose.

"In this desolate and lonely land," he says, "the majesty of the storms impressed on the beholder a sense of awe and solemn exaltation. Tossing their crests, and riven by lightning, they gathered in their wrath from

[97]

every quarter of the heavens, and darkness was before
and under them; then, in the lull of a moment, they
might break apart, while the sun turned the rain to silver
and the rainbows were set in the sky; but always they
gathered again, menacing and mighty,—for the promise
of the bow was never kept, and ever the clouds returned
after the rain. Once as I rode facing Kenya, the clouds
tore asunder, to right and left, and the mountain towered between, while across its base was flung a radiant
arch. But almost at once the many-colored glory was
dimmed; for in splendor and terror the storm strode in
front, and shrouded all things from sight in thunder-
shattered sheets of rain."

After the rains are ended and the long dry season sets
in, the animals depend more and more upon the scattered water holes which like magnets draw them over
many dusty miles each day. As the heat increases and
the skies remain blue and blazing, the water level sinks
a little lower every twenty-four hours. When the pans
or holes are so depleted by evaporation and by the thirsty
herds that they are in danger of drying up altogether,
the animals in the vicinity begin to decrease as they mi-
grate in search of other drinking places. Almost at the
moment that the last drop of liquid disappears from the
muddy bottom of the holes, nearly all wild life vanishes
from that section of the country. A place that a little
while ago has been extremely populous now rapidly

Adventures in the African Jungle

takes on the aspect of a deserted country. Then not until
the storms again fill the air with thunder and pour down
the rains will the wild creatures return to overspread the
land. 32410

While Carl and I were hunting giraffe in northern
Kenya, we witnessed this drought and its attendant mi-
gration. Because of it and because necessity is the mother
of invention, my husband evolved a plan to keep the
game within the neighborhood of our camp—a plan
that to my knowledge had never been tried before.

So long as water had been abundant, giraffe and the
other animals native to the region were plentiful; but,
with the diminished supply, they began to move away
in search of greener pastures. This was a twofold disappointment. Because we had spent two weeks in looking
for a particularly fine giraffe for Carl's museum group,
it was now heartbreaking to see them leave before we
secured the specimen we sought. Again, one of our chief
pleasures during spare moments was to watch and study
the animals that came to drink at a water hole near our
camp. Both our serious business and our sport were
therefore about to be spoiled by the lack of water.

One morning my husband had an original idea. He
would rebuild the water hole! Perhaps the game would
come again to drink. Taking with us a dozen natives,
each bearing sharp *pangas* (knives), he set them to work
scooping out the hole to a depth of eighteen inches.

[99]

Adventures in the African Jungle

In the excavation Carl placed a large linen tarpaulin, covering the edge carefully with some of the clay that had been removed in the digging. Then he filled the freshly dug pan with water from an old saline well near our camp after making sure that it was safe to do so. The chief of the Samburu—native herders who grazed their flocks near by—told us the well held an inexhaustible supply of water but, to prevent all possibility of cutting short the amount required for our daily use, we tested his statement by baling out a quantity of water and then watching to see whether it would come again to normal level. The well filled so quickly that it must have tapped an underground stream far below the earth's surface. Satisfied that it would flow sufficiently to satisfy our needs, and also supply enough for the experiment, we carried to our improvised water hole more than a hundred gallons of the precious liquid.

On the day following the building and filling of the artificial pool, our excitement was intense. Would thirst lure the herds back again? The success or failure of our practical test would be decided within a very short time. We hoped, watched, and waited.

In the morning a fair number of antelope and zebra came in and drank. That was encouraging. We hauled out more water and kept the pool well supplied. Then we set out on our regular daily search for giraffe. As the hours passed, belief became conviction—something was holding our long-necked friends. It even seemed that they were more numerous than they had been on the preceding day. By evening it had become certain that the game in the district had scented the water and had decided to remain. Our venture was a success!

We were tremendously elated, and at sunset Carl came to me with eyes shining.

"How would you like to sleep by the water hole to-night?" he asked.

"Would I? Just give me the chance," I replied.

He had pulled together an old thorn blind that had been used three or four years before by Blayney Percival—and reconstructed it within a few yards of the water pan. At twilight, when ready for the night's adventure, we prepared to take our position in the blind. It was about the size of a small stack of curing hay—such as dot our American meadows at harvest time. We got down on our hands and knees to crawl in but found it would not do. The entrance was too small to permit even that humble posture. So, throwing ourselves prone on the ground, we squirmed and wriggled our bodies through the narrow entrance. It was neither easy nor comfortable. The walls were like so much barbed wire, lacerating our heads and backs. And the earth was strewn with thorns which pierced our hands and knees. However, torn clothing and scratched skin were not important enough to stop us. We had come to see, and to hear

Adventures in the African Jungle

the practical working of an experiment, and nothing else mattered.

With sharp native knives we cut three peep holes in our shelter. One was for Carl, another for me, and a third for the eye of the Akeley motion picture camera. Placing our guns within easy reach, for use in case of emergency, we quickly spread out a canvas sheet and unrolled two heavy blankets. There was a crisp wind blowing from the snowy summit of Mt. Kenya and the night was sure to be cold. Then, blocking the doorway with a heavy thorn branch, we settled ourselves to wait for the opening act of a night of jungle drama.

It was after eight o'clock by the time we were ready. Our thin sweaters were doing duty as pillows, and our ears were so close to the ground that the vibration of every approaching footstep could be easily distinguished. As it was improbable that any animal would come to drink so early in the evening, my husband advised me to 'catch forty winks,' saying he would do the same.

Carl went to sleep almost immediately, with that enviable ease which was always a marvel to me. Lifting myself ever so little on one elbow, I could look out and see the water hole and a bit of the surrounding country. Nothing stirred. Perhaps the next few hours would witness queer shapes and strange actions about our shelter, but for the moment it seemed an earth without sign of life. The night was moonless. Only the stars cast a faint glow over the gray veldt, lessening the darkness of the great mysterious plains. Inside it was pitch dark. I could barely distinguish the outline of my husband's head two feet away from me. The sound of his light breathing was lost in the stirring of the fitful night breeze that cast an occasional twig against our thorn enclosure, or shook down on us the dead grass from the weaver birds' nests in the table-top acacia overhead.

Only a slight stretch of the imagination, and I could have believed myself utterly alone by the water hole in the quiet and darkness of the early African night. I shivered. My spine was prickling. Foolish of me to let fancy run away with me and yet—all the magic of a strange continent was about me, and all the familiar things of daylight seemed to have vanished into another world. I was frightened much as I used to be when as a very little girl, my father would send me out across our long back porch to the well under the dark grape arbor for a pitcher of water. I shivered now just as I had in those childhood days, when facing the darkness beyond the light and peace of my mother's sitting room where for me always dwelt safety and a refuge from every harm.

As the moments crawled along, the very air seemed freighted with the tenseness of approaching events. We, the hidden watchers, knew that our experiment was successful—but we did not know what adventures it might involve. Miles away, thirsty beasts had scented the water. Through the bush and across the plains, nostrils were dilated, sniffing the wind to catch the direction of our improvised well. Many feet were moving instinctively and steadily toward us. Eyes—gentle or fierce—were guiding their owners closer. We were being surrounded by a tightening ring of wild creatures.

What action would the next few hours bring forth? Were we destined to witness fierce enemies do battle with claw and tooth? Would we ourselves be compelled to struggle for our lives? Our blind could offer but little protection against the assault of an angry beast. If a charge were launched by an enraged or frightened animal we would have no choice but to face the attack. Our retreat was cut off by the very thorns that sheltered us.

Still I supposed, the chances were that we would not be discovered and that my husband believed that there was small possibility that any of the larger and more dangerous animals would visit us. In that country the dangerous beasts were the lion, the elephant, the leopard and the rhino. And of them all, the rhino, the blundering, charging, unthinking rhino, was far and away the one most to be dreaded because here he was the one most prevalent.

In the semi-blackness before our 'front-row' seats, the show was now beginning. In that half-way house between sleep and conscious thought, I sensed the approach of the first actors. I felt the slow, steady pressure of my husband's hand on mine. Suddenly I was wide awake, realizing that for a long time I must have been in the borderland of dreams—dreaming that I was afraid. I was stiff in my shoulders and the arm I had been using as a pillow was quite numb. Carl was kneeling with his eyes at the peephole. Something was certainly happening. The patter of light feet resounded on the baked clay outside. Quickly and quietly as I could, I got on my knees and crawled to my own lookout. It was possible to see a little outside in the star light of the great constellations overspreading the vast domed sky.

Small, shadowy shapes gathered about the brink of the water hole—Grant's gazelle. Among the most beautiful of all antelopes, their graceful bodies merged and blended in the faint light like a fantastic moving cloud. Next came the clatter of many zebra hoofs—heavy, rhythmic, like the galloping of mustangs—and the Grantis were driven from their recently discovered treasure. The harsh deep call of the Grevy zebra stallions was unmistakable. Snorting and gulping, they took immediate possession of the water hole. A half dozen oryx soon followed, trotting in leisurely and drinking with the zebra, in the same friendly manner in which they are accustomed to graze together in their pasture lands. They are so well matched, in size and strength, fleetness and fighting ability, that there is no conflict between them. As though blessing Carl's improvised water hole, they guzzled and talked to each other. Maybe they wondered at their good luck, but it is more likely that they simply accepted without question that which fate had brought to them.

Soon they stopped drinking, sniffed and snorted a little, and then made off across the veldt. The echo of their hoofs was still audible when we heard a new and distinct sound. We crawled nearer to our peep-holes—scratching ourselves anew with the thorns, in our eagerness to watch the entrance of this important actor. A huge leaden shadow loomed out of the greater shadow of the night. A most extraordinary noise now began. Snorting, pawing, gulping, grunting, guzzling, the newcomer made himself entirely at home in our water pan. It could not survive long, the way the big fellow was trampling it about. Only one creature could be guilty of such bad manners—old rough-and-ready rhino.

Suddenly a hyena set up his doleful yodel, and jackals ran barking into the night as the shambling monster came into our line of vision. Beheld under such circumstances, the rhino was even more strange, more reminiscent of some prehistoric monster, than he had ever been when viewed in the sane sunlight. He was like some phantom in a dream, with his incredible head and astonishing bulk etched against a faintly illumined world.

Apparently our huge visitor did not suspect that he

was being observed. Several times his ugly snout and vicious double horn were pointed straight in our direction, but the rhino, unlike almost all other animals, acts as if he were wholly unafraid, and never resorts to the caution and wariness practiced by many other beasts. There was little possibility of his seeing or hearing us, as a rhino's eyes are not of the keenest, and he was making too much noise himself to detect the faint sound of our movements. Still, there remained a strong likelihood that he would get our scent. If that happened, trouble was headed our way. Our interest and excitement were too great to let us worry about a little thing like a couple of tons of rhino, and apparently he was too content with his discovery of the water to bother about any humans who might possibly be in the neighborhood. Into the pool he ploughed and splashed—head, foot, hoof and hide!

Unfortunately the rhino is not a dainty drinker, and our visitor seemed determined to live up to—or down to—the reputation of his family. While he drank he wallowed, and while he wallowed he ruined our beautiful water hole which had been built with so much labor and care in the hope of keeping the game near us for many days. We watched this operation with mixed emotions. We were altogether willing to have an opportunity to study this great beast unobserved and at such close range, but we could not help feeling sorry that our

Adventures in the African Jungle

smaller and more polite friends would find nothing on the morrow but a muddy mess when they came in for their morning drink. Their disappointment would be ours as well, for they would immediately leave the vicinity of camp and we would see them no more.

Our nocturnal visitor was making a great display of his careless strength, and each of his clumsy movements added to the havoc he had wrought. Occasionally he came quite close to our hiding place, and with his monstrous body only a few yards away it was not difficult to realize that he was capable, in an idle moment, of destroying us with as little effort as he had employed in wrecking the water hole. Despite these disagreeable possibilities, we watched his maneuvers with as much interest as if our thorn thatch were a bomb-proof—or rhino proof—dugout.

To make the story properly thrilling I suppose I should say I was 'paralyzed with fear' or 'frozen with horror' at the imminent chance of his charge. But at the expense of losing an opportunity to feature the 'dangers of Africa' I must confess that I thoroughly enjoyed that hour spent in watching the heavy antics of the rhino, and I was less concerned about my personal safety than I have often been when merely crossing the traffic-flooded street of some American city. To be sure, my confidence in my husband's knowledge and experience, and in his ability to protect me and teach me the ways of the country, was like a strong wall between me and fear. And my confidence was perpetually justified.

As for our friend, the reprobate rhino, he left us as unconcernedly as he had come. Just as the thin horn of the ancient moon falteringly climbed into the sky, an hour or so before dawn, he ambled off to his favorite pastures, there, doubtless, to gorge his water-filled stomach with the dry and dusty forage of the veldt.

Behind him he left but the sorry wreckage of our experiment. It had worked—and worked well—but its life had been very short indeed. Compared to a rhino in such a bath tub, a 'bull in a china shop' is a gentle household pet. We were convinced that no more animals would come to the hole and that, if by chance any should arrive, they would depart immediately after one swift sniff at the scene of devastation. We waited a while and our fears were justified. Our pool that had been so promising a few hours earlier was now anything but a tempting drinking place.

When the east grew faintly streaked with dawn, giving us a better view of our surroundings, we crawled out of our thorny refuge, startling a colony of golden feathered weaver birds in their nests in the acacia overhead. A whirr of wings, a skyward rush, and the hornbills, roosting near the pool, took to flight, their over-sized beaks opening to emit their harsh and jarring cries. We were just in time to disturb a flock of sand grouse drifting in to seek the water that had slaked their thirst the day before—this time, alas, only to find destruction and disappointment.

All the way back to camp the plains were dotted with the friendly little wild folk who had given us our night's entertainment—antelope, zebra, oryx, soon to vanish in the perpetual quest of water. They, too, had enjoyed a new experience, had they but known it, in drinking from a man-made water hole.

My cook had cups of steaming tea awaiting us when at length we reached our tents. After putting our torn clothing in the mending bag and scrubbing up for a hot breakfast, we were ready for the day's work. Rather than depleting our energy, the night's experience had stimulated and invigorated us. We set out after giraffe with fresh determination—a determination which carried us through until the following day when the big giraffe, for which Carl had hunted so patiently for more than two weeks, was obtained. To secure such a splendid specimen was a notable achievement, but our night at the water hole was one of the most enjoyable interludes in all the time we were on the trail.

When I think of those happy, work-filled days in Africa, days in which we could at least pause at eventide and rest without anxiety or deep concern, I would that the hands of time might backward turn and that again I might share with my husband the thrill of spending a

Photo. by Carl Akeley.

THE WATER HOLE MAY BE A RENDEZVOUS OF FRIENDS OR THE BATTLE-
GROUND OF HEREDITARY ENEMIES.

night on the stony ground in a thorn blind beside our improvised water hole—that once again I might share his keen delight in glimpsing and in listening to the wild folk in that bit of unspoiled Africa, as they reveled in the gift to them of my husband's ever deft and labor-loving hands.

CHAPTER VI   MONKEYS AND BABOONS

BY MARY L. JOBE AKELEY

It was eight o'clock—a clear, crisp morning in the highlands. We were traveling slowly through heavy timber. A yellow aureole was over all the tree tops. They swayed and whispered as tiny waves of air ebbed and flowed. Big spots of gold decorated the massive silvery and white tree trunks brightening now and then the long sweepers of gray-beard moss. Masses of reddish-purple fuchsias glowed like banked-up fires far back in the sylvan gloom. Here and there, where the golden splotches fell, little greenish-yellow animals—chameleons—moved and paused and blinked and loved the wine of life. They traveled on perhaps seeking greater warmth and straightway became the color of the trees they were clinging to. All along the wide trails worn smooth by the great Tembo, the sunshine struck and soothed and warmed. Everywhere else the shadows were thick and dark.

All at once a great commotion arose in the jungle.

[112]

Adventures in the African Jungle

Something was happening way up among the higher sun-lit branches. There was much rattling and banging about, and then the little people of the forest began to talk. Suddenly we saw who they were—a band of Sykes' monkeys in full action. They were out for a lark! For all the world as if they were playing the game of 'follow the leader,' they swung from one bough to another, making almost a 'bee line' through the trees.

One young fellow, a bit too ambitious for his size, lost his hold and tumbled to earth, but in an instant he sprang off the ground and was up and at it again. So quick was he that he fell behind only three of his fellows. The mad skirmish kept up. Now a dozen were in full sight—and there must have been six times as many more judging from the racket. How amazing are these little monkeys! Quick as a flash, up and away from danger in a second, they are the incarnation of freedom, the spirit of the untouched jungle. Perhaps, sometimes, a help-less baby, lost or motherless, may require man's protec-tion, or on some rare occasion one of these little animals may be needed for scientific observation. But how anyone might wish to capture one of these childlike creatures merely to *own him as a pet* is beyond my power to understand.

The monkeys were now traveling right along the fringe of our wide elephant trail. Of course, their extraor-dinarily sharp eyes had spied us long ago. They were no

Adventures in the African Jungle

longer relying as forest dwelling animals usually do, for protection in concealment. We kept very quiet. They slackened their pace and watched us intently. We hoped they knew how friendly we were. For a minute we were conscious of being thoroughly inspected. Then they dashed off again, as if at the drop of the flag, now racing through the lower branches of the trees. Surely they were out for a holiday! We had an excellent view of them. They were dark bluish-gray, with such a lot of red points on the hair of the back that they, too, looked as if gilded by the morning sun. On the under part of the body the hair became lighter. It looked as soft and fluffy as fur. The Sykes is indeed a handsome little animal. Fortunate were we in having this 'close up' of him, because as a rule he is so timid that you see a movement in the branches—a flash of grayish gold and that is all.

We now came to a full stop, waiting in the trail in the hope that the rest of the band would come into view. A large flock of noisy gray parrots calling and screaming at each other suddenly darted down into the very midst of the monkeys. Then something big and definite happened in the forest. Trees crashed a dozen yards away. Suddenly the air was torn and rent by the most soul-stirring of all sounds—the trumpeting of elephants. Then all was still. Parrots and monkeys stopped mute. We remained rooted in our tracks. Not a sound came from the dark breathless forest. After what seemed an eternity, old Tembo trumpeted again, but this time far away. He had not got our wind. The elephant's shriek, receding into the distance, now came to all of us as a note of reassurance. In a little while, the monkeys began again. They tore along screaming and chattering as before. We too pushed on in the hope of keeping up with them, but their pace was fast. Perhaps, that morning they had tired of their usual fare in this their haunt on the edge of the forest. They may easily have been off on an early raid to rob a near by native *shamba* or to plunder the crop of some hard working white settler in the cultivated fields below us.

Certain it is that these sturdy little fellows find themselves in their element no matter whither they are bound. Just as easily as they accustom themselves to the palm thickets in the lowlands of the sea coast, so here they find a perfect home in the high and frosty uplands under Africa's eternal snows. That morning we had no doubt that they would be on easy terms with any job of looting they might undertake. And as the last monkey tail flashed by we found ourselves wishing them good luck in their escapade.

*   *   *   *   *

A fortnight later, we were in camp at The Wells, north of the Northern Eusso Nyiro. On every side stretched out the wide, parched veldt. Our tents were pitched be-

Adventures in the African Jungle

side a sand river—a roaring flood in the wet season, now so dry you could walk across it everywhere. Over us the wide branches of table top acacias cast a vague and delicately patterned shade. Their blossoms were sweet and pungent. Innumerable insects reveled in their perfumed hearts. The bees buzzed so loudly I decided to leave my tent where I was writing at my diaries and go out to watch them as they worked to store up treasures for the natives' honey hives.

Just as I walked outside my doorway, I caught a glimpse of something large and dark moving among the trees on the other side of the sand river. I looked and at first failed to locate anything. Then, as my eyes grew accustomed to the brilliant sunlight into which I had suddenly stepped, I saw not one but several figures gliding along the ground in the midst of the high stalks of hibiscus, red and yellow with many brilliant flowers. Three or four of the creatures soon climbed carefully along the almost horizontal and low-growing branches of the misshapen vine-hung trees. It was a band of monkeys coming in to pay us a welcoming call.

A small group now posed on one of the nethermost branches. Near the tree trunk sat a mother, her baby hugging her about the neck. Next to her were two half grown monkeys of a light rufous color, while near the end of the heavy limb where it turned abruptly toward the ground sat the old man of the family, just like a sentry on guard. He was a handsome fellow, twice the size of the female, and with dark and white markings about his heavy shoulders. He must have weighed sixty pounds. This family group gazed steadily in my direction. I slipped back to my tent, secured my field glasses and thus had an excellent opportunity to observe them. There was little doubt, from their markings and behavior, that they were a troop of Patas monkeys.

Scampering about among the vines and grasses were several more youngsters. Two of them were particularly daring. They soon capered down to the edge of the sand river and then, at sight of me, scurried back to their original position. Next they took up their post together behind a large tree. From this vantage point they began to play hide and seek with me. One would peek out on one side and then draw his head back quickly while his brother would poke his head out on the other side. You could almost imagine they were whispering to each other about me. Presently, another young animal joined them. More daring than all the rest, he stepped quite openly out on to the soft sand. Obviously he did not like his shifting footing any too well, and so he took it rather gingerly. As he advanced toward me, he looked back every three or four steps, as if to see whether the others were as brave as he. At last, when midway across the sand river, he sat down and stared intently at me. The whole band apparently never had seen anything so strange before. I began to feel embarrassed. Soon the youngster, having satisfied himself with gazing at me, walked down the river bed a little way and there he hid behind a tree. From that vantage ground he began to inspect the cook, from whose kitchen savory odors were being wafted to him on the breeze.

Presently far up along the bank of the river, and beyond the group still watching from the low-growing branch, appeared half a dozen mothers. Each was marching along with her baby riding pig-a-back and holding on to her neck for dear life. Their late arrival looked for all the world as if they had been unable to keep up with the rest of the procession while carrying their heavy infant load. There were probably fifteen or eighteen all told in the troop. The monkeys had attracted the attention of no one else in camp, and I watched them, without shifting my position, for a good half hour. Not once did they give any indication of fear or excitement other than great curiosity.

Now these monkeys behaved very differently from the ones we had recently seen in the Kenya forest. They did not seek the high branches of the trees. And when they climbed on to a limb they went up slowly and deliberately and were never more than six or eight feet from the ground. Even the young ones seemed not particularly inclined to climb trees but for the most part kept up their antics on the ground. Their arms were very long and they traveled rapidly and securely over the loose gravelly earth. Apparently they were quite at home in the midst of open, rough, thorn country, a great many miles away from any dense cool forest.

In about an hour the last monkey had vanished. Early the next morning, I was alert and watching for their return. Presently several little faces appeared in the vegetation on the other side of our sand river. I stole out to my observation post of the previous day, where I was half hidden behind a little thorn bush. The monkeys were back again, sure enough, but this time there were not more than half a dozen. They stalked about in plain sight watching me, not from behind trees as they had done the day before, but now quite fearlessly. After a brief quarter of an hour of inspection they left the place for good. We remained in that camp for more than a month, but the monkeys never revisited us; and, although we were constantly traveling to and fro through the bush and over the open thorn country of the northern plains, not another monkey was sighted there. I always hoped they might return to visit me, and often wished I might have found something to lure them back again, but their curiosity must have been completely satisfied.

* * * * *

I was driving my husband's heavily laden lorry back to Kenya with our Congo collection. We had spent the entire morning climbing to the summit of the Uasin Gishu Plateau. At noon we had reached the highest point. Feeling a bit chilly in the shade, while we ate our lunch, we had put on our top coats before getting into our cars again. The sun was welcome indeed in the crisp cold wind of this nine-thousand-foot altitude.

Our motors had just started on the long down grade, through vast wheat fields turning golden in the mellowing sun. These cool uplands are indeed white man's country! Here and there flocks of iridescent Jackson's dancing birds with long curving tails, floated over the ripening wheat.

Beyond the cultivated lands we suddenly entered a bamboo forest. On either side, tall, closely growing canes rose in an almost impenetrable wall of green—a sudden and striking contrast to the open country through which we had been traveling. Since I was eager to be in camp, and because there were still many miles to go, I was getting the best I could out of the old lorry with its ton and a half of freight. Suddenly, Bill, in the seat beside me, and the six other black boys, topping the load, began to shout. There, dead ahead of us and in imminent danger of being ridden down, six Colobus monkeys were crossing the road.

On either side of the track the bamboos were shaking, where the remainder of the troop fed upon the feathery leaves. I jammed on my slack foot brakes and seized my hand brake and, while my top-heavy load skidded sickeningly to one side, a great grandfather Colobus flashed and flattened himself out a few feet in front of my big machine. The old fellow was making a desperate effort to escape. His companions in the bamboos shrieked in terror. By almost a hair's breadth the animal made the opposite wall of green. The long hair of his brilliant black and white coat gleamed like strings of jet and ivory.

Whether the creatures had been attracted by the hum of my motor and had come out on the road on a tour of inspection, I can only guess. More likely they had grown tired of one patch of bamboo and had taken just that moment to change their feeding grounds.

The Colobus monkeys are all too popular a prey to both beast and native. While in the tree tops they are constantly in danger from eagles, and when they seek refuge in the undergrowth, the most terrifying of all their enemies, the leopard, is on their trail. Like other monkeys, they chatter away at a great rate as they travel about the trees looking for tempting morsels of juicy leafage. Whenever frightened, they raise a great commotion, crying out so loudly from the depth of their lusty lungs that they can be located easily by either talon or claw.

Some natives have the same barbarous taste that a few of our 'civilized' fur wearers have. They covet the gaudily marked monkey pelt with its long silky hair, and they go to great extremes to hunt these children of the forest with their dogs. It is said that a large male Colobus is no mean adversary. If in the chase he is shaken out of the trees in which he seeks safety in rapid flight and is finally brought to earth, he puts up a hard and unrelaxing fight to the finish. I am more than thankful that there were no casualities in the little troop that crossed my path and that I can recall without regret that crisp December day on the Equator when I both saw and saved my first Colobus—the most beautiful monkey in all Africa.

* * * * *

We were sitting at dinner one evening in the Lukenia Hills. Two days before we had pitched our tents in broad meadows filled with flowers and there my husband and I had established our first home in the African blue. Several times before, on his early expeditions, he had seen in this same spot a great abundance of game. Although the land was now green and blossoming after the heavy rains, yet there was little sign of wild life anywhere. From our high camp ground we could look out on every side to the deserted plains over which the game had once so freely roamed. Suddenly, as we sat at our table, under a wide open dining fly, my attention was attracted to the summit of a near by *kopje* (bare rocky

Adventures in the African Jungle

hillock, literally 'a head') sharply outlined against the sky. Something had altered it—it was higher and differently shaped, or else my eyes were playing tricks. I ran for my glasses. Returning, I noticed my husband smiling at me. His trained eyes had seen that which required my binoculars to reveal to me. The sharp black 'point of rock' which had suddenly crowned the *kopje* in the failing light was nothing more or less than a big granddaddy baboon, surrounded by three or four females. He had perched himself on the highest rock of all, and they had gathered around him, all bent on seeing who had invaded their domain. As I dashed to my tent for my glasses, I may have excited the animals, for now the old man began to move back and forth quickly along the narrow ledge while he gazed in our direction. His manner, suggesting resentment and curiosity, reminded me of a grizzly bear I once had seen high on a cliff in the Canadian Rockies. As our pack train had passed through a narrow gorge a few rods below him and parallel to the rock ledge on which he stood, the old grizzly had paced up and down, greatly disturbed at our nearness. On two successive evenings the baboons appeared on their high lookout. Their activity and their interest in watching us never abated. They were the first baboons I saw in Africa.

Baboon collecting for one of our groups was a part of our program. But here in Lukenia the animals were so few that my husband was unwilling to take even one of them. By contrast, when he had been in this region fifteen years before, they had been so abundant that they frequently made the night as well as the day resound with their noise and particularly so when either a leopard or a cheetah stalked them.

A few months later we were in the Lower 'Ngourmetti in Western Tanganyika. It was evening and a heavy thunder storm was brewing. Red flashes of lightning were splitting the low, boiling clouds. My husband and I had been photographing giraffe all afternoon. It had been an unusually tricky job, because the plains were soft from recent rains, and once or twice our photographic car had almost stuck in the mire. Heading toward what looked like better going in light bush country, we found firmer ground. Our chance to reach camp before the storm would break seemed fair. We had just rounded a clump of bush, when we came face to face with a big grandfather baboon challenging our approach. He did not give an inch, and he looked as savage as he must have felt. Streaming up along the rising ground were forty or fifty baboons, all making a rapid get away into the thicker bush above. The old fellow was growling at us in seven different languages, and looking as ugly as any human when enraged by some intruder. Our chugging motor and our voices had disturbed the animals in their own country. We turned out of the way of the old soldier so courageously defending his band, but as long as we were in sight he remained there vigilant. There is little doubt that he would have shown fight had we pressed him in the least.

It is said that the old male baboon neither has affection for the young nor is he actually on good terms with the whole band. In fact, he seems to have an habitual grouch, so far as his family life is concerned. But let any danger threaten, then he will show his responsibility by standing ground between his troop and any peril. If it comes to a showdown between himself and any other animal, he will fight to the absolute finish.

A few days later one of our porters, Kambi, rushed up to me in great excitement. He had been with us from the beginning of our expedition. Like all the other boys of the *safari* he knew it was my first trip in Africa and was always eager to show me anything new and amusing. Kambi was a Wanyamwezi, and here, in his own country, he knew what to expect in the matter of animal life. He signaled me to follow him quickly. Not more than a quarter of a mile from camp we came to a high *kopje* rising abruptly from an almost level plain. The rocks were bold and rugged, and over and about them grew a tangle of beautiful vegetation, literally alive with baboons. I have never seen so many before or since. The topmost rocks were filled with them and they trailed all down the sides of the *kopje* on to the plain below. There were certainly more than one hundred.

We went up close to the animals. Most of them were munching away at something and making an awful row while doing it. Our nearness disturbed them so little that we were able to approach within a few feet without annoying them. But in a little while the nerves of the old male leader got on edge. He set up a great racket, and the rest of the band followed his example. Then he rushed up to the tiptop of the highest rock and there challenged our presence. He evidently had a bad opinion of us and made no attempt to restrain his feelings. He finished his tirade with a succession of angry, deeptoned barks. There was no question but that this old male was ready to defend his household to the last ditch and with savage effect.

The baboon's attack is always a terrible thing. His jaws are strong and his teeth are powerful. When he bites he tears out mouthfuls of flesh. No man would enjoy a hand-to-hand encounter with an enraged, full-grown male baboon. Although baboons, like monkeys, dread cheetahs and leopards—both formidable enemies—it is a well-known fact that an old male baboon has courage enough to pursue and even attack a cheetah which has threatened his household.

So far as the old male on the *kopje* was concerned, I

Photo. by Carl Akeley.

SYKE'S MONKEYS LOVE THE SAFETY OF THE
GREAT KENYA JUNGLE.

THE OLD FATHER BABOON DID NOT GIVE AN INCH,
BUT GUARDED HIS RETREATING FAMILY.

A GRANDFATHER BABOON.

Adventures in the African Jungle

felt rather uncomfortable at arousing such emotions and provoking such an outburst in the poor beast, but the porter, Kambi, only doubled up with laughter. He was having priceless entertainment at the baboon's expense. Meanwhile, all the baboons except the old male were making off across the plains, to some scrub a few rods away, beyond which arose another *kopje* perhaps half a mile distant. They traveled on the double quick. The mothers retreated in close formation. Their little ones— some were very small indeed—rode on their necks, hunched up like miniature jockeys riding to the finish of a race. The mothers were going fast—one entirely too fast, and her little baby lost his hold and down he fell violently on the ground. He jumped up and did his feeble best to overtake her but he was a groggy little thing and could hardly run. She slackened her pace but did not stop for him until they were both some distance away. Then she waited long enough for him to mount again. Some young males took their time to it, carefully covering the retreat of the females.

It is a well-known fact that the mother baboon is very gentle and tenderly affectionate with her offspring. When her baby is newly born she carries him underneath her. When he grows older he rides on her shoulders. Mother baboons also show great affection for the young of such domesticated animals as dogs and cats.

Not only do baboons eat the wild vegetation, but on

occasion they will pillage native corn fields. Sometimes when the moon is bright, they make their raids at night, getting perhaps as much sport out of it as does the small boy who plunders the pumpkin patch on Hallowe'en. They will also rob birds' nests of eggs and nestlings. But, strangest of all, baboons search out and eat scorpions, one of the most poisonous insects with which a man can come in contact. At this same camp in Tanganyika where Kambi showed me the baboon parade, my cook was badly bitten by a scorpion. He suffered intense pain and nausea for a day and a night and was several days in recovering. The scorpion stings by striking with the sharply curved spike at the end of his long, elastic tail; but the clever baboon, before eating, seizes the end of the scorpion's tail and in a flash pulls it off and then stuffs the animal into his mouth.

The nerviest little baboon I have ever seen was near this same Tanganyika camp. My husband and I had gone out to hunt a lion for our collection. It was to be a little holiday for us since we had been working very hard for many weeks. In a valley which had not been hunted in before, we found all the animals quite unafraid. We soon came upon a large number of baboons moving in the tall grass. They were as inquisitive as the monkeys that ran chattering about among the branches of the trees and they were far less shy. The whole troop of baboons stopped to look at us for a long time; a group of young

Adventures in the African Jungle

ones climbed up on a half fallen dead tree. A mother, with her little one beside her, sat on a tall stump. After a while she jumped down, and he, attempting to follow, fell headlong. She soon leaped back to her original position and the little fellow clambered up after her. But he lost his hold and down he went again into the tall grass. Up again he scrambled, and after several attempts he finally succeeded in balancing himself on the tree stub, where he sat watching us until we disappeared.

But my most intimate experience with a baboon was when I found myself in full charge of a baby baboon and quite without my seeking it. It was when my husband, who had been ill of fever, was recuperating in a private hospital in Nairobi—the Kenya Nursing Home. Rockwell, completing his collection of baboons and other animals to supplement the Klipspringer Group, had been spending several weeks in the Kidong Valley. There baboons were far more plentiful than in Lukenia where, owing to their scarcity, Carl had been unwilling to kill any.

Having finished his work, Rockwell had brought his *safari* back to Nairobi. I happened to be at our base house the morning he arrived. Sitting beside him on the seat was his gun boy, Molimo, a large, handsome Masai, six feet tall. And in the big native's arms was a pathetic little mite—a baby baboon—perhaps two or three weeks old. It was almost hairless and its pinkish body was covered with brown blisters, crisped in the hot sun to which it had been exposed. His mother, supposedly a solitary female, had been taken for the collection. So tiny was her baby that, as he snuggled down in her thick hair, he had not been visible to the hunters.

Molimo was laughing loudly as he brought the baboon to me. It is strange how young primates will cause the native so much mirth. Molimo promised me that he would care for the frail creature in his own quarters and give it warm milk to drink.

My hands and my mind were too full at that time to think anything more about the baboon until two days later, when again I was in our Nairobi *shamba*. Near the servants' quarters I heard a wailing sound like the cry of a very young infant. I went into the tin building used as a storage room and there on the cold cement floor was the little baboon quite collapsed beside an open can of condensed milk. It was thus the black gun boy was caring for the little animal.

When the baboon saw me he renewed his wails. His eyes were bleary, his body scabby, and he was shivering miserably. There was nothing to do but gather him up, wrap him in a piece of old blanket and put him in a native *kikapu* (little basket) and take him down to my room in the Nursing Home. There I gave him a few spoonfuls of sweet, warm milk and greased his mangy, fuzzy little body. He looked like the proverbial 'drowned rat,' but

Adventures in the African Jungle

he cuddled down in his blanket and soon went to sleep where I placed him in the sun. When he awoke he was so lively that I took him in to Carl's room to show him my new charge. I shall never forget the look in my husband's face—

"Where in the world did you get that baboon?" he asked.

I told him.

"Well, you had better find a home for him quickly, unless you want to keep him for good," he said.

I had heard of a monkey that had once attached itself to his *safari* and had become the occasion of great responsibility for him. He had told me that, under no circumstances, would he ever have another such pet near him again.

"If you keep that little beast three days, you'll be tied to him for life," he said.

"You'll find him as persistent and demanding as a child, with all the child's pains and problems—only he won't be able to tell you about them."

I knew I had to arrange for the little baboon's future, and also that I had to take care of his present. Placing him in his basket on the front seat of my car, I drove down to a shop and secured for him a proper nursing bottle and a piece of flannel for his blanket. Then I carried him back to my room and fed him again. He demanded nourishment 'every two hours,' sleeping between times as any good baby will. As I was constantly needed at the hospital except when doing important errands in some brief period during the day, the care of the baboon was easy enough.

When bedtime came I fed him again, putting a hot water bottle in the bottom of his basket, and soon he and I were fast asleep. But at one o'clock the baboon's screams awoke me. I switched on my light and there, beside my bed, stood the little fellow shaking and shivering and yelling. I jumped out of bed and wrapped the baboon again in his blanket. There was nothing but a little cold milk for him and no way to heat it. Of course, he refused to take it. Tucking him back securely in his basket, I turned off my light, in the vain hope that the baboon would be quiet. But no sooner had I settled down than the baby, squirming himself free from his blanket, again stood screaming by my bed.

Now, on one side of my room was my convalescent husband greatly needing all the sleep possible, while on the other was a mother with a three days' old infant. Knowing full well that it was no place for a howling baboon, and terrified lest he waken one or both of the near-by patients, I seized the pathetic creature, wrapped his sticky, smelly body in clean 'Americani' (muslin), and jumped back into bed with him, putting him well under my blankets. He seized my shoulder in both his babylike hands and clung to me as tightly as if I were his mother. In a moment he stopped sobbing and shivering and soon was warm and snoring. Whenever I moved he clung to me for dear life but he cried no more throughout the night. It was thus I found myself nurse-maid to the baby baboon.

Next morning he clamored for his bottle and, after gurgling at it for ten minutes, he became as spry as anything. He jumped all about my room. He scratched his head thoughtfully while I combed my hair, and when I put him out in his basket in the sun, he would have none of it but began to play among the flower beds. I fastened a broad belt of soft muslin about his middle and to that attached a long leading string which, in turn, I tied to his basket handle. He could just move the little basket and thus was free enough for his happiness and at the same time was safe from straying off.

After midnight that night and also the next night, the little baboon slept with me. I began to realize most forcibly the truth of my husband's advice. And I also began to be worried. What should I do with the little animal? All the black boys, except my personal boy and Bill, had gone on leave and I scarcely wished to employ a nurse for the little shaver. But luck soon came my way. That very day Mrs. Philip Percival came in to see us. On her estate at Potha, thirty miles away, she had four or five half-tame female baboons. In the great kindness of her heart she volunteered to take the little animal and let one of her baboons mother it. Well aware that it was at least a 'baboon's sized job' and a constant one at that, to look after the little fellow properly, I was by no means unhappy to see the baby ride away, clutching his nursing bottle and snuggling close to the neck of one of Mrs. Percival's black boys.

Six months later, on my return from the Congo, I went down to say farewell to the Percivals, and incidentally I saw the baboon. He had grown to be a fine little chap, weighing perhaps ten or twelve pounds, and was in the pink of condition. His long silky hair was golden brown and shining. No longer was he an object of pity. He was now the proud possession of one of the largest female baboons. After all his misfortunes he had found a happy home at last.

CHAPTER VII   CAMPING IN AFRICA

BY MARY L. JOBE AKELEY

IN almost every respect, camping in the African wilds is different from the camping we know in the north woods or in the snow-capped mountains of America. In the Western World you have delighted in the joys of sleeping in a bed of fresh cut spruce or balsam—of carrying a twenty or thirty pound pack over steep rocky trails —of loitering at noon full length in the refreshing shade of flower-filled alpine meadows, cooled by glacial winds—of plunging your travel-stained and weary body into a deep pool of clear, cold water when the sun is half way down the western sky—of drying off in the sunshine. You have come into camp as the evening shadows lengthen feeling as hungry as a dozen wolves and like the proverbial 'million dollars.' And still you have had energy enough to chop wood, light your cook fire and make coffee and broil bacon; in fact, you have loved being a general factotum or 'camp hound.'

Adventures in the African Jungle

You have known all these joys of the gay, free life in the open, but by the same token, once you are in Africa, you will find yourself practically without any real experience whatsoever for camping as it is done on the Equator.

I make one important exception—as applied to my own case. The resourcefulness I had gained by my ten expeditions in Western Canada, prior to my marriage, stood me in excellent stead in the matter of the problems I was required to solve on my first journey to Africa in 1926. My mountain climbing, my connection with scientific expeditions in Northern British Columbia, my ability to execute that 'last long mile' when I was nearly 'all in'—all these experiences gave me a mental and physical hardihood and a fund of practical knowledge which proved invaluable when I was required to cope with affairs of the out-of-doors and of the people, black and white, with whom I came in contact. I was very grateful for this asset in my thirteen months of active service on our expedition in the African jungles.

In Africa the word *safari* has several meanings. It may simply mean *camp*. You look across the shimmering plains where there was nothing an hour ago and you see a glint of green canvas and the drifting smoke of a fire and you say, "There is somebody's *safari*." Again, on the march with a dozen lorries and automobiles rolling along and with columns of dust obscuring everything but the chugging noise of the motors, you say, "There is

Adventures in the African Jungle

someone's motor *safari*." Or, if you see—as you rarely do nowadays—a long line of black boys on the trail, each with his head load, and perhaps marching in time to a drum or native chant, you remark, "Somebody's *safari* is on the move." Then, when you are planning a trip or an expedition into the field, you say, "We shall go on *safari* at such and such a time and to such and such a place." *Safari*, therefore, may mean the material outfit; the total personnel, with outfit, on the march or in camp; or it may mean the expedition itself.

Usually, here at home, we have chosen to sleep in white canvas or balloon silk tents. In fact there is something picturesque and inviting in a group of white tents pitched against a background of green forest and reflected in the blue, limpid waters of lake or stream. But in Africa you shun white canvas as you would a deadly plague. Only the black porter uses the cheap white cotton tent. The white man selects in the best London outfitting establishment his tents of sea green linen—so dark that to a great degree they exclude the sun and cast a refreshing shade, in a land where shade is scarce. They are so durable that they will not rot in the combination of the heavy downpours of the rainy season and the fierce and bleaching sun that inevitably follows. They are so well prepared that they will not mildew and decay even when soaking with rain they are packed and transported in the sun. Always a grateful protection

[137]

while the land is sun-scorched and waiting for the rains, they become a haven of refuge in the wet season, affording the distinct feeling of the luxury and security of a little home.

On cool and windy nights, when you are tucked under your thin Jaeger blankets and your mosquito canopy, your tent becomes a safe retreat. Again, on the rare occasions when you do not go instantly to dreamland, your tent is snug and cozy as you read yourself to sleep by the fitful light of an oil lantern swinging from the metal tent pole near by.

Occasionally, beasts of the jungle prowl about your tent. Sometimes when adventuring in the wilds a lion may drive a herd of zebra almost to your door. A leopard may skulk about, looking for a juicy feast of native mutton or even craving an unsuspecting black boy. An inquisitive, hungry hyena may be out on a night hunt for refuse. But, more often, a far more deadly enemy—the Anopheles mosquito—is lurking about, ready to poison your blood with malaria. In any case, your green tent, tied up at the bottom and ventilated near the top when any possible danger is afoot, your finely meshed English bobbinette mosquito net, ninety-nine nights out of one hundred, will be the safeguards of your mental and physical peace and security.

In British Columbia I have spent scores of nights in the open without tent protection. Sixty nights at a stretch

Adventures in the African Jungle

I have slept dreamlessly, my sleeping bag rolled out on Mother Earth, without even boughs for a mattress and sheltered only by a branching spruce or by the starry coverlet of night. In thirteen months in Africa I slept only two nights on the ground—and those were nights when the extremely hard and long day had left us no time or strength to make a proper camp; when, in fact, we were 'all in' and ready to fall in our tracks. There is a popular belief that it is harmful to sleep on the ground in Africa—that certain vapors exude from the earth throughout the night—that it is an easy way to contract fever, and so on. Whether this be true or not, it is certain that a comfortable, canvas Gold Medal cot, full three feet wide, and equipped with a three-inch-thick kapok mattress, is a first requisite for safety and comfort on your *safari* life. Occasionally, in our expedition base in Nairobi, we had the added luxury of an air mattress protected by a cotton or wool padded covering. But for the most part, I rested sublimely, night after night, in my little canvas cot, without any spring or 'give.' I came to love it, almost as I had loved the hard ground in the early years of my camping in the West; and when at last I returned to a proper bed it seemed both strange and uncomfortable.

The tropical tent has a floor cloth of the same material as the tent itself. This is attached to the walls of the tent, at ground level, by means of heavy hooks and eyes, so arranged that there is an overlap of canvas thus excluding creeping things. All told, I have seen only three snakes in Africa. One of them—a puff adder—chose my abode in which to spend the night. My black boys found him in the morning under the ground cloth when they struck my tent.

Once on a long back packing trip in the Canadian Northwest every member of the party had to carry his own dunnage. It meant cutting absolute necessities down to the very last ounce. I even broke off the handle of my tooth brush, placing it in my pocket and using the smallest of combs which I wore in my hair. My one and only silk pocket handkerchief I washed each night in a glacial stream after it had served me as a towel. I do not recall having any soap. Our individual dining equipment consisted of a cup and a spoon and a jackknife. Later my guide paid me no uncertain compliment. "Mary Jobe carried her thirty pound load all the way during our climb," he said, "and for ten days *she was just as dirty as a man.*"

Now, in Africa, there is seldom reason for any member of the *safari* to be as 'dirty as a man' for any length of time. Many an evening when you come in from a long trek on foot or when you have driven your heavily laden motor a hundred miles over the dusty plains, you might easily be mistaken for a native, your face is so brown and travel stained. But nine nights out of ten there is a chance for at least a 'teacup bath' and for a change of linen.

When on *safari*, it is not always easy to find a suitable site, affording wood and water sufficient for a one-night camp. Of course, there are occasional rest houses along certain well-known routes. But the rest house itself you always avoid as a sleeping place, since there is no way to tell who has occupied it previously or whether its shady recesses harbor some of the disease-breeding ticks. It is an invariable rule that you pitch your tent a fair distance from the rest house, using it or the semi-open grass *banda* (shed) near by as shelter only for your dunnage. In the spacious and often stockaded grounds surrounding these rest houses, you will find sun-cleansed and rain-washed grass fit for your tent site.

On motor *safari* you often stop just in time to make camp before sunset. Again you may camp after night if you have looked long for a favorable site or if you are intent on mileage. If darkness overtakes you, there are two ways to find a camp site—to go on until you reach a stream near the track and then, with your searchlights, locate enough ground for the placing of your cots; or to inquire of the local natives, whom you usually find in numbers near the watering places, as to where a proper camp site may be found.

When you draw near a native village, your approach is always heralded as if by some unseen messenger. Just as you turn off your motors and loosen your tarpaulins covering the loads, the local natives troop in carrying large earthen water jugs filled to the brim and bundles of faggots borne on their heads.

Making camp in dry country is another matter. If you are going into an arid region and you have received any idea of it from those who have been there before you, you must always safeguard yourself by carrying a large supply of water. Fill your old petrol tins and lash them on the side of your motors, or, if you are on foot, load them on your porters' heads. Once I was forced to carry firewood as well as water. It was when I started on the three-hundred-mile journey from Tanganyika to Nairobi, with my husband ill of fever and in his bed in a large motor truck. The fall rains had been threatening for a long time and we had had one heavy shower. After traveling two hours, we were overtaken by a severe storm. Our trucks were stuck in the mud. We could not turn a wheel even by putting on our chains. Using the dry wood I had brought with me, we lighted a fire after the storm had passed. Without this supply we would have had a sorry time, as the only wood about us was green timber, and my husband required hot, nourishing food. The water we carried proved an essential also, as we were mired down far from any pool or running stream.

Five weeks before, when en route to Tanganyika, we had made another dry camp. I had been driving my car all

CARL AND MARY AKELEY IN THEIR NAIROBI GARDEN. WITH THEM THEIR HALF-WILD CAT.

Photo. by Carl Akeley.

AT DINNER IN THE DINING TENT OF THE AKELEY-EASTMAN-
POMEROY EXPEDITION IN THE LUKENIA HILLS.

Photo. by Mary L. Jobe Akeley.

SOON AFTER REACHING CAMP THE LOCAL NATIVES APPEAR
BEARING LOADS OF WOOD AND WATER.

Adventures in the African Jungle

day after having worked until past midnight the night before packing for the trip. As usual I drove at the head of the procession. My husband soon noticed it was difficult for me to keep my car in the track. I was actually having my first go of African fever, with a temperature of 102°. He knew I was not well, and so decided to camp as soon as possible. We accordingly stopped near a *donga* (gulley) where there was plenty of dead wood. But I doubt if there was any water within a radius of eight or ten miles. Again our 'debbies' (tins) of water were put to good use.

Occasionally you get a big surprise when you place your tents in some friendly spot which you think is just suited for a delightful camp. Perhaps it is near the summit of the Uasin Gishu Plateau or in one of the little draws leading up along some mountain side. Such a camp we had half way down the Eastern Escarpment where the motor road descends into the Kidong Valley.

Just before dinner, I had noticed that our cook was having trouble with his evening fire. Every now and again sudden gusts of wind blew away the coals from under his cooking pots. At bedtime the breeze had stiffened perceptibly. On coming in to camp I had asked to have my cot placed under a fly stretched from my husband's little tent over to his motor load. I keenly desired to sleep in the open because I had been very hot all day. It was a perfect spot and a perfect night and I wanted to go off

[143]

to dreamland watching the bold black hills against the starry sky. It all went very well for an hour after the camp had settled down. Then the wind began to blow so hard that my canopy lifted and boomed and fell for all the world like a wet sail in a keen blast. There was no sleep for me under such conditions. I loosened the shelter and tucked it securely into the motor and then sought refuge inside the tent. The wind was so high and so cold that I would have been chilled and uncomfortable indeed had I remained in the open all night long.

Wherever you camp in Africa it is an invariable rule that you must choose the highest and driest ground, away from any deep shade. One of the worst illnesses my husband ever had was in the early days of his African experience when he camped in the shade of heavy-leafed trees by the river's edge. It was a cool, grassy spot, such as one would invariably choose in America; but in Africa it held one of the white man's worst enemies—the fever-breeding spirillum tick.

As soon as your canvas is unpacked your boys begin to clean off your camp site. If you plan to remain there several days, they are careful to cut all the long grass, to pull up the roots, and to remove any hummocks. You may thus have a level place for your bed and chairs and a smooth footing under your ground cloth. Our black boys took a keen pride in the appearance of our camp ground. With our long experience in camping we were both

Adventures in the African Jungle

'dragons' about having them bury cans and burn all
refuse and keep our camp site perfectly clean. They
rose to the occasion, as they always do when you mean
business.

In Africa there is never a time when you plunge into
a stream for coolness or refreshment. You may be jolly
glad to have your boy bring you a basin of hot water in
the morning and place it in the wash stand. A tiny canvas bathtub full of the same mud-tinged liquid for your
evening bath is not always possible as a daily luxury, but
if you should camp by a large river, like the Northern
Eusso Nyiro, you will have an abundance of water. However do not go in swimming—in fact do not walk too
close to the brink of such waters—or you may not finish
your *safari*. The crocodiles are there, too, and they are a
hungry lot with all their teeth sharpened and their
mouths watering for a taste of you. When you get back
to your expedition base in the town, you may have a
pukka (proper) tub bath. But even that is not always satisfying, because you realize that a tub one-quarter full is
all that you should allow yourself in decency to your fellow men, since water is so generally scarce. Some time I
shall camp on a large African lake—Victoria or Kivu or
Tanganyika—and indulge myself completely in the extravagant use and waste of water.

If building fires and swinging an ax and 'toting' water are necessary to your out-of-door happiness, do not

make the mistake of going to Africa because there you never do these things. Your porters, whom you pay sixteen and two-thirds cents a day in United States currency, are employed to do all menial jobs; and if you were to be seen slimming your waist and hardening up your muscles in such vigorous tasks, you would lose caste with your black boys. You never make your bed nor pack your dunnage nor do your laundry. Your tent boy does all these things for you. Sometimes, if you are extremely tired and he is a very kind and thoughtful tent boy, he removes your shoes and stockings, too, and bathes and massages your aching feet. For such service you are outwardly, but sparingly, grateful—allowing him to consider it an honor rather than a servile task. But inwardly you bless him.

So far as ordinary cooking is concerned, this you never do unless your cook is so untrained that his food is unfit to eat. You may, in fact you *should*, order every meal. It is necessary, unless you have that rare jewel of a head boy who is clever at catering and at the same time honest and who will relieve you of this often irksome task. I have heard rumors that such boys exist. In fact, I have seen one of these capable creatures in action—but I have never had such a boy in my employ. In any case you rarely enter the kitchen. That is the cook's domain, and it is sometimes just as well for your appetite that you do not know too much about what happens there. But when

Adventures in the African Jungle

you wish to contribute some new dish or a delicacy that will brighten up the menu, be sure to prepare it on the dining table and only supervise its boiling or baking at a respectful distance from the cook's fire.

The laying of the dining table, the laundry of the table linen—for you actually have snowy white table cloths—and the serving of the food, are the duties of your personal boys. If well trained, they are quick, neat, and quiet. In our base house in the town, they usually wore clean, long, white robes—in the Mohammedan fashion—and appeared at time of serving at table with covered heads and bare feet. On *safari* it was necessary to forgive them their heavy hobnailed boots in which they always made a great clatter, because even their horny-soled feet were not proof against the ever present and penetrating thorns.

When time comes to break camp, the headman and the porters strike and pack all canvas and, under the master's supervision, they load the motor lorries. Now the motor *safari* has made serious scientific work, sight seeing, and big-game hunting in Africa less difficult than formerly, just as it has also destroyed much of the romance of the wild. With three or four lorries and twenty native boys, you can accomplish in three or four months the work it required two years to perform under the old regime of porter *safari*. You are up bright and early. Camp is broken quickly. All your outfit is arranged in convenient

[147]

bundles and boxes and the loading begins. If you are to be away from your base of supplies for two months, you put all reserve equipment and stores on the motor body first, so that they be not off-loaded every night while in transit. While the lorry is being packed, you must see to the safeguarding of precious camera boxes and all semi-perishable goods. Finally, a large tarpaulin is placed over all and lashed down. It reminds you a little of covering the load of a well-cinched and heavily laden cayuse with a pack mantle and then, as a last formality, of throwing the diamond hitch.

It was necessary to have our loads, which would be needed the moment we arrived in camp, placed at the rear of the motors, so that they were the first thing our boys would naturally lay hands on. In this way they were quickly and easily accessible. I invented red and blue symbols for the speedy identification of these loads. The markers, which looked like big Chinese suns, struck the fancy of the natives, so that they were very seldom misplaced. On porter *safari*, the loads which the cook first required in camp, such as pots, pans, kettles and food boxes, were carried by the boys who led the procession.

The personnel of an African *safari*—motor or porter —consists of black boys of various ranks who command varying wages. Chief among these is the *neapara* (head-man) who has much of the problem of transport in charge. He receives one hundred shillings or more a

Adventures in the African Jungle

month in East African currency and, like all the rest, you give him in addition his *posho* (food). Usually when on *safari*, this *posho* is rice but in the town you give him cash, varying from one-half shilling to one shilling.

The *neapara* supervises the making and breaking of camp. He is responsible for the porters, who receive as wages twenty shillings a month, and who perform the menial work of camp. They do the packing. They run the fires. They cut and carry wood and bring the water. Their *posho* on *safari* is usually corn meal or mealy meal as it is called, or it may be dried beans, bananas or sweet potatoes. In the town they receive one-half shilling for their food and spend it as they wish. As a rule, porters are of the lowest class, uneducated and primitive. Seldom do they know more than a word or two of English. Frequently, however, they are the most reliable, trustworthy and honorable of all the natives you may have in your employ.

The cook is a high priced boy commanding from seventy shillings to one hundred shillings per month. Sometimes they are extremely good cooks; frequently they are mediocre; often, poor. Under the cook is a *toto* (kitchen boy) who builds the fires, washes the pots and pans and receives a porter's wages. Often a clever cook makes his *toto* do much of the cooking, while he stands by or sits smoking away at his cigarette as if he had no care in all the world. Thus the *toto* gets an excellent training.

Adventures in the African Jungle

Occasionally the apprentice becomes so expert that he does his chief out of the real job and becomes the cook himself.

The tent boys look after your personal needs. They care entirely for your tent, your dunnage, and your laundry. If your boy is a Mohammedan, he is unrelaxing in his desire to wash your clothing. Unless a garment is put definitely in a place in which your boy knows it is ready for immediate use, he will carry it away and wash it. On the whole the results are satisfactory. They rub your clothing threadbare, using an extraordinary amount of soap, but it is always very clean. They use a large iron, similar to a tailor's 'goose,' the heating of which is accomplished by placing hot coals in an inner receptacle of the iron itself. To one accustomed to wearing rough-dry clothing, as is usually unavoidable in camp, well-ironed garments are indeed a luxury.

Your tent boys also serve at table and wash the dishes. Sometimes they sew and mend neatly. On one occasion, I found the need of using an extra sun canopy since I was working for a good many consecutive hours in my tent. I had several pieces of material, one of which I tied in place above my head. But about every half hour, as the sun climbed upward in the sky, I had to stop my work and readjust the canopy. Finally, Makasudi, our headman, noticed what I was doing.

"I'll sew you a big *hema* (tent canopy)," he said.

Adventures in the African Jungle

I laughed at him—I thought he was joking. "You give me big needle. You give me big thread. I show you," he urged.

I produced the needle and thread, and soon Makasudi was enthroned on a high rock in the shade of a tree sewing away as skilfully as any tailor. He enjoyed my astonishment hugely and grinned and chuckled every time I looked his way. He did an excellent job and I was protected for many a month from the fierce rays of the African sun.

Every base camp employs *askaris* or guards. They are usually ex-soldiers who perhaps have seen military service in the Great War. Sometimes they are taken out into the field. Our expedition artists always had their *askaris* at hand, as guards or gun boys, thus allowing them complete freedom for their work. When all forces go into the field for a day's work, the headman is left in charge; or if the headman is required in the field, the camp may be left in charge of an *askari*.

Most important as members of a scientific expedition, are the gun boys. If intelligent, experienced and well trained, they are beyond price. They can save their masters much detail. They clean and oil the guns and place them carefully in their master's tent at night. If on motor *safari*, they put the guns aboard in a safe, convenient and regular place. If on porter *safari*, the gun boy carries the heavy gun which is adequate for ele-

[151]

phant, buffalo, or lion. He never goes far from his master's side. When shooting and two guns are employed, the gun boy is right at his master's elbow, ready to pass the second rifle and reload the first when discharged. A *real* gun boy has distinct ability as a tracker. Some are born trackers—invaluable in case of following spoor or a wounded animal—others have inferior ability. In any case, no one 'on his own' in Africa should be without the best gun boy obtainable.

Your natives always listen to the voice of authority. They loathe lackadaisical orders. They deride any master lacking in courage. Treat your black boys tenderly and they rise up and mock you; give them definite and intelligent orders and they respect you. They quickly sense a bully. They expect and thrive on fair treatment. But do not coddle them. Do not look on them as a 'downtrodden' race, unless you wish to merit their ingratitude and their insolence.

It is amazing how thoroughly a *Bwana's* (master's) reputation envelopes him. A native will go far for a man who plays the game fairly, and whose judgment is superior and without question; but let any expedition leader—man or woman—once show weakness, meanness, cruelty or indecision, then his position with his black boys is lost. If a leader fails to command homage, his black boys will become disobedient, rebellious, hostile, and, in times of crisis, may be guilty of desertion. The rank and file of ordinary boys enjoy that discipline which holds them strictly to account. They are unhappy when allowed to slip and slack. They thrive under personal and definite discipline and happy is the man or woman unafraid to correct when punishment is merited.

No matter how strict you may be with a native, I believe that you need never fear physical violence, so long as you are just. They detest being disciplined by a woman. Under such conditions they become the laughing-stock of all the *safari*. Their companions invariably side with the *Memsahib*, and life is made irksome indeed for the culprit. In the old days the *kiboko* (whip of hippo hide) was used liberally on all occasions when punishment was required. Now it is used sparingly and in only the remote parts of the British dominions. Those who are supposed to know are inclined to the belief that a fair amount of corporal punishment has always been of great value in the development of the native's character. It had at least the effect of making him 'want to be a good boy,' and, as long as he knew he might expect corporal punishment, even a boy inclined to be bad was apt to remain a good member of the community. But now in many places an employer must take an unruly, ill-intentioned or even a dangerous boy to the law court where he receives his discipline only if a case is proved against him. While waiting for trial, the boy can often be guilty of similar offenses and of insufferable cheek.

Adventures in the African Jungle

If the case is adjudged in the boy's favor, he will some-times go forth inclined to stir up sedition on every hand. In one of the government posts of Western Uganda, where the *kiboko* is still in fashion, the District Com-missioner told us he had an almost universally law-abiding native community. We camped there for several days. The courtesy of the natives, the quiet of the post, the immaculate order of the grounds, all bespoke the best of local government conditions, whether the *kiboko* was a potent factor or not.

With so many black servants, it might easily seem that a white woman on *safari* would have very few occupa-tions left to her—in fact that she might easily become bored with herself and with life in general. As an integral part of my husband's last expedition in Africa, I was not only secretary of the expedition but I was constantly with him in the field—driving cars and trucks, for all transportation, for collecting and for photography. In addition, I was the general camp factotum or *safari* man-ager. As such, I first 'signed on' all the boys—arrang-ing the wages at which headman, gun boys, cook and personal boys were employed. I also 'signed on' all our porters. For all of our employees I prepared records of employment and dismissal—a report required monthly by the District Commissioner at Nairobi. Then I kept accounts of wages earned and paid and of money drawn in advance.

Adventures in the African Jungle

Once, Mwanika, my cook, out in our camp in the Lukenia Hills, wished to buy two cows from a Wakamba herder. I had to advance two months' wages which amounted to about two hundred shillings. As a formality, I secured a receipt and a signed agreement to give me a lien on his cattle if he quit my employ before he should have earned the full amount. To Mwanika this purchase was a momentous affair. I was willing to oblige him, because he was a pretty decent sort as well as an extraordinarily good cook. I was certain he would go into the sulks if I did not render him this favor and I knew his cooking would suffer. But this cattle deal consumed at least three hours of my precious afternoon, the greater part of which was spent in Mwanika's telling me how excellent the cows were, what a 'good buy' he was making, and how greatly he desired them because his wife and child needed the milk. Finally he stated that he was sure that they would cost twice—maybe three times as much—in Nairobi.

A harder-hearted person than I—I had been only three months in Africa at the time—would have granted the justice of Mwanika's request. Thereafter, in the same camp, he came to me four or five times asking for shillings that he might buy, for his own use, native fowl which the Wakamba brought in for sale. Mwanika's cash account was thus somewhat intricate and always a thing of importance.

Adventures in the African Jungle

This cook was a thrifty soul and I quite delighted in his shrewdness. At last he confided in me that he had a little *duka* (shop) of his own in the straw-thatched native village on the outskirts of Nairobi. One evening, when in the town, he told me he needed supplies from home and begged me to drive him down to his village. Sitting beside me and as excited as any school boy going home on a holiday, he gesticulated at every crossing, guiding me through a maze of narrow streets, and finally told me to park in front of the open window of a tiny shop. Without waiting for me to stop the car, he sprang out, rushed into the hovel, and in a moment brought out a very pretty young native woman, whom he introduced as his wife. She was immaculately attired in white—trim and smiling. After seeing her I had greater faith in the cleanliness of Mwanika's cooking than I had ever had before. Next he carried out a very tiny and very squirming bundle and proudly pointed to the little brown face with eyes bright and blinking in the light of my motor lamps. It was Mwanika's first baby. But his great exhibit was his little *duka* (shop). It consisted of a few bins of mealy meal, rice, beans and sugar, a dozen tin cooking pots, and several cartons of cigarettes and matches. That was all. "I make fifty shillings profit here every month," my cook asserted boastfully. Thrifty Mwanika!

In camping, your routine is frequently interrupted by the unexpected. In fact, each day has a varying program. For example, you may be camping so near a tribal village that you will inevitably share some event of great moment in the lives of the natives. I recall one day when all hands in camp were at work preserving specimens. Suddenly a dozen Wakamba herders appeared, each carrying a spear or heavy club. They were greatly excited. They gesticulated wildly; their usual soft voices were raised to a high pitch. One half-grown boy was weeping loudly, his oily face smeared with tears. As usual, Bill was sent out to learn the cause of this outbreak. He came up to the tent where Carl and I were at work and somewhat amused, related to us the story he had heard. He told us that there was a huge snake down in the tall meadow grass of the valley below us. The Wakamba had said that the big snake had eaten their favorite dog. In fact, it was by far the best dog they had, because he was so skillful in herding their cattle in and out of the *manyatta* (cattle pen).

Carl told Bill to take my .275 Hoffman gun and go with the Wakamba and kill the snake. After an hour or so the whole procession marched back into camp headed by Bill. Behind him walked four boys, each carrying the end of two long poles they had lashed together with a strong rope-like vine. On this improvised stretcher, and borne aloft, for all the world like an ancient sacrifice, lay the big snake—a great python. He was twelve and a half feet long and weighed close to eighty pounds—

exclusive of his evening meal. His scaly body, strangely patterned in brown and black and white, gleamed in the sunshine. But he was not a really handsome snake because in his middle was a huge bulk—a fifty-pound dog. Immediately behind the stretcher walked the Wakamba youth—the owner of the dog. He was chief mourner. His lamentations grew louder and louder the nearer he came to us.

The snake was quickly dissected and the dog rescued. Of course, he had long since ceased to breathe—but otherwise he was quite intact. The boy's howls now rent the air. Poor fellow! He doubtless had loved the unfortunate mongrel just as much as you or I have loved the favorite collie or wire-haired terrier of our childhood.

The python was photographed both before and after his evening meal was taken away. Then he was skinned and skeletonized. We thus obtained unexpectedly a valuable and interesting addition to our collection.

The African python is the largest of the constrictors, but it is almost certain that he confines his depredations to the smaller animals such as duikers and the lesser gazelles. The best authorities agree that he, like almost all wild animals, is inclined to give man a wide berth. One day, several months later, I was traveling by lorry in one of the most remotely wild parts of Tanganyika. I heard a peculiar rustling sound in the grass at one side of

Photo. by Mary L. Jobe Akeley.

THE TWELVE FOOT PYTHON AFTER EATING A WAKAMBA DOG.

Photo. by Mary L. Jobe Akeley.

NATIVE TOTOS (CHILDREN) ARE AS INTERESTING AND LOVABLE AS OUR LITTLE TOTS AT HOME. SOMETIMES THEY ARE MORE INDUSTRIOUS.

the track. A huge python literally whizzed across the roadway, no doubt startled by the buzzing of our motor. He went probably twenty yards, and then made a dash for a low-growing tree, entwining his body around a leafy limb, almost entirely concealing himself. One of the men took a hasty shot at him and missed. The python quickly made off for 'parts unknown.'

When the python sets about his business of obtaining his supper, he first pounces upon the animal, catching it in his coils and then crushes it to death or insensibility. Next he begins the eating process. He swallows the animal whole, first surrounding the most manageable portion of the creature with his large and elastic mouth and then actually pulling his upper half including his stomach, completely about his prey. The whole carcass is now in the python's stomach. For the next day or so digestion continues, the snake remaining for the most part stupefied and motionless. The Wakamba dog, although it had been 'eaten' perhaps three hours before, showed no sign of disintegration.

As I have said elsewhere, I saw only three snakes during more than a year in the field. After my return to America, a girlhood friend of mine said, "Well, I suppose Africa is almost entirely a vast forest with snakes hanging down from the limbs of nearly every tree." This false idea of the wilderness and of the dangers of Africa is due to the fact that from time immemorial many adventurers have wished the world to think of them as *heroes*. Therefore, even today certain travelers are prone to paint the African wilds as a place of horrors with danger lurking at every turn. Thus often by word of mouth, by motion picture caption and by the printed page, fictions are broadcast, and the credulous accept these statements as unvarnished truth.

Another all-too-frequent incident of *safari* life—an episode frequently crowning the day's events—is when the chief of the local village brings to you a retinue of 'lame, halt and blind.' Knowing that every important *safari* carries with it a first aid kit, and since the majority of African natives are usually widely separated from any medical assistance, the chief appears asking for *dawa* (medicine), perhaps for one of his sick wives, for his children, or for some of his subjects. Nine times out of ten he brings the invalid with him even when the sick person is so ill that he has to be carried, perhaps for a long distance. This pilgrimage to your camp marks the beginning of a very active clinic. Fortunate it was for me, and perhaps for them, too, that I had had a considerable experience in first aid and in the practical nursing of children.

One of the most pathetic moments I have ever experienced in dealing with natives was in our camp on the Northern Eusso Nyiro, when the Samburu chief brought to me one of his ailing wives. She was a pretty, delicate thing, her face distorted with suffering; and so frail was the woman and reduced by fever, that she could barely stumble along behind her husband, with the aid of two of his other wives. Right in the middle of camp, she fell in her tracks and lay prone in the path between my tent and the dining quarters. Her husband approached within a few feet of where I was working and stood there, insistently eying me and muttering something I could not understand. Finally my personal boy told me that this broken creature was the chief's youngest wife, that it was most important that the *Memsahib* cure her at once. Carried by one of the other women, was the sick wife's tiny infant—not more than six weeks' old. His wails, as the hungry little fellow demanded his helpless, moaning mother, intensified the touching scene.

What to do in the case was indeed a grave question. "*Gonjwa sana*" (a great pain in the stomach) I was told. It was easy for me to see that she was having fever. The usual simple remedies—salts for the sick stomach and quinine for the hot head—were all in safety I dared give her. The chief looked his concern. He thanked me very much. He also hoped very much indeed, he said, that my *dawa* would work a speedy cure. The poor creature stayed in camp until sundown and then the natives slowly carried her home. A week later, I had the satisfaction of receiving a special visit from the chief. He came to tell me that his wife's fever had left her and that the little *toto* (baby) no longer cried all through the night.

Foregathering round about the outskirts of this same camp, came other natives—men and women. They all had very sore feet or fingers, caused by poisonous, piercing thorns. Frequently, the thorn had broken off in the injured member which had become badly festered. These embedded thorns had to be removed and the ordinary treatment for infection given. Again, natives with sore eyes came for aid. They were a most unpleasant sight, being attended by swarms of small black flies. Boracic cleansing was all I dared attempt, being cautious to wash my hands in disinfectant before and after treating the sufferers.

Half-grown children seldom were found in the ranks of the afflicted. As I saw many of them playing about their villages, they seemed a sturdy lot, bent on mischief and frolic, just as they should be and like all the other little children of the world. I often thought what a great advantage these little people had over their fair skinned brothers, since here they wore only the lightest of garments—a bit of soft oil tanned goat or sheep skin—and they were for the most part constantly in the open, whether at their play or at their small tasks of herding the flocks.

Another hectic moment of African *safari* life is when

you want to take your expedition from one governmental district to another. It is then necessary to obtain permits for the transportation of all servants, as well as to comply with the customs regulations necessary for carrying supplies from one colony to another. In addition, if you are on a hunting or collecting trip, it is also essential to secure the proper hunting licenses from the game warden of the colony to which you are going. It may all seem a simple procedure, but it is not. It involves much effort and detail; and when you come back to headquarters, many of your boys go on the rampage and are late in appearing at your base. They are half dead while on duty, owing to the riots of pleasure they have been enjoying in the town.

Your black boys constantly afford other diversions. When a boy is ill or injured, or even homesick, he demands no end of attention. They are always asking for salts and quinine. But when a boy wounds himself with his *panga* (native ax), when he is injured by any other sharp thing about camp, such as the metal stripped and lined chop boxes, or even when he runs a poisonous thorn two inches or more into his callous foot—then indeed the *Memsahib* of the *safari* is in immediate demand. No child could run more quickly to his mother than does this black boy dash to you for help. Your first aid job is cut out for you. Many a long, sinewy black leg I have bathed in bichloride and dressed in antiseptic salve and gauze day after day, lest serious infection occur and a valuable boy be permanently disabled or even lost. They are all babies —craving your ministrations, whimpering and groaning considerably while at the dressing stand, and often sniffling and weeping when the cauterizing becomes painful. After the dressing is finished, they loiter around waiting for a compassionate word or smile and seldom leave without it. All of our black boys were stalwart men in their prime. Some were six footers. Many of them were hardened rascals of the deepest dye, lazy, guilty of petty thefts and falsehood, given to wrangling amongst themselves, yet they demanded of me, with the insistence of any white child, my full measure of assistance and of sympathy for their ills. I confess that my woman's heart was all the more touched because of this display of childish weakness.

But when a white member of your *safari* becomes sick, it is another story. Then it is a rare boy indeed who will permanently give a hand. After six months of arduous field work, my husband lay seriously ill of fever in Tanganyika. We had spent the most strenuous month of all in photographing lion spearing, followed by 'playing with' fourteen friendly lions. Added to this, had been the hard work of collecting, in the remnants of the day, a group of plains animals. In the crisis of my husband's serious illness, it was only Bill who rendered me real assistance. On duty as I was, all day and every night until midnight, it was Bill who took the watch in the last half of the night, thus making it possible for my strength to last throughout this period of danger and anxiety.

Kombo, my husband's excellent tent boy, did his regular tasks with care, but never was he inclined to put in that 'extra pound' so greatly needed in our long pull for Carl's recovery. At this time, I had a young and untrained cook, whose cooking had always been bad enough. Now he seemed to ruin everything and I had to prepare every morsel of food so that my husband might be tempted to eat enough to keep him from failing utterly. It may have been my imagination but the cook seemed to run amok. Finally, after our three-hundred-mile journey in a motor lorry, my husband was installed in comfortable surroundings in the Kenya Nursing Home in Nairobi. With complete fidelity, Kombo settled us both in our rooms and arranged our dunnage. With my husband's improvement under the care of a good doctor, I began to breathe more easily. The burdens seemed to be lifting. But the next morning Kombo appeared with bloodshot, streaming eyes, sniffling away at a great rate.

"My mother," he said, "is very, very sick. She will never get well. I must go to her *shamba* and take care of her at once."

I was promptly sympathetic. Kombo's appeal was not to be denied. But as I was signing him off, since he insisted I should do so immediately, I caught a shrewd look

Adventures in the African Jungle

in Bill's eyes. I wondered what it meant. When Kombo had departed, sobbing and mopping his eyes, Bill began to grin, saying, "You know, *Memsahib*, Kombo never have any sick mother. Kombo only put red pepper in his eyes so he cry easy. Kombo never want stay with any sick man. Kombo never want to help care for *Bwana*." Wise Bill, I thought. Black Kombo had completely pulled the wool over the unsuspecting *Memsahib's* eyes!

In Africa, your day is never long enough. When you are out continually in the field, on a job of photographing or collecting, the time for household chores has to be lopped off your hours of sleep. It means getting up at three-thirty, jumping into mosquito boots and dressing gown, routing out cook and boys, coming back to your tent to splash some water on your face and dress for the day. Then you hurry into the dining tent, where by lamplight you see that the table is properly laid, for your personal boys are sleepy indeed before daylight, and knives and forks all look alike to them. Next you give your cook his supplies for the evening meal and, with him, plan the menu. As you do this, you collect the lunch needed for a day in the field. You now see that the others are called, that they have a basin of hot water to open their sleepy eyes and that morning pick-me-up— a cup of hot tea. You stop long enough to drink a cup of tea yourself. You make sure that all the water bottles are filled with drinking water from the canvas water coolers, for each member of the field party, and that the felt covers have been soaked in water so that, by evaporation, they may remain cool for several hours.

As all your companions are now drifting out of their tents, you urge your cook and boys to bring on the coffee. You dish out the stewed dried fruit, and the opening ceremony of the day is in full blast. On with the bacon and eggs! One boy stumbles over a tree root and another rescues the platter. But somehow the breakfast is served and eaten. Finally, when the men are lighting up their cigarettes, seeing that guns, skinning knives and taxidermic paraphernalia are all in place, that the tanks are filled with petrol, the radiators with water, and that plenty of extra 'debbies' of water have been loaded on, you dash over to your tent, clap on your sun helmet and jump into a light sweater—because the air is still keen and cold—grab camera and extra film box and hurtle into your seat at the wheel in time to limber up your cold motor a little while the men are climbing aboard. Then, just as the night fades, and you can barely see the track in the faint green light of dawn, you head your lorry out on the veldt. You crush down masses of big, white moon flowers gleaming with dew and, long before the coming of the sun, you reach the grassy pockets near some quickly diminishing water hole where the game herds have washed their dusty throats throughout the peaceful night. And so a second chapter in the day begins.

Adventures in the African Jungle

You now have nine or ten hours of hard hunting, in the blazing sun, with a brief respite for lunch at noon in the doubtful shade of a thorn tree. The hunt is by no means ordinarily crowned with success, for the demands of a collector-naturalist are great indeed, and hunting from six to sixteen days for an excellent specimen is the conscientious way to play the game. You may, therefore, return to camp bringing with you the satisfaction of a splendid trophy, dearly earned; but much more frequently you bring back discouragement and often despair. In any event, when the day is finished, you are almost finished too. You are tired—dog tired—in every bit of your mind and muscle. More likely than not, when you reach camp you are met with a tale of woe. Some boy has nearly chopped off a toe; the *posho* is all out; the bread just would not bake that day; all the drinking water has been used in cooking, and a motor now has to be sent to the river ten miles away; the Somali's camel *safari*, that camped a little way off the previous night, stampeded just as they were packing up, and half knocked down your tent and the dining fly, and one of the camels ate your very softest, thinnest pair of pajamas. Or the Samburu dogs came in as the pudding was cooling in the shade on the dining table and, while the boys were taking their afternoon siesta, they were awakened by the clatter of pans and they had found the

[168]

dogs licking the basin clean. Certainly it had not been anyone's fault, and they had stoned the dogs, and they would never trust any food to cool out in the open again. And of course *Memsahib* should know that was not all, for the same dogs had cleaned up all their *biltong* (smoked meat) where it was hanging out drying in the sun—and had the *Bwana* shot anything today? And they had very much hoped he had, because they now greatly needed *nyama* (meat) especially so, since there was no *posho*.

Now, these are the joys of 'countless servants' in Africa. Believe it or not, under such circumstances, I have more than once fallen into my canvas chair absolutely all spent, and have let my black boys rattle on for full fifteen minutes, resolutely closing my ears to their outpouring and giving them such a vacant stare that they must have known I was not listening. Finally, in seeming pity, they would leave me—returning soon with hot water for my bath. After that Christian ceremony, and I was again dressed in clean, loose clothing, and had slipped my aching feet into my precious light-weight mosquito boots, I would saunter over to the dining tent, there to begin to unravel the maze of petty troubles in the hour left before the dinner gong. Oh yes! 'You always take a siesta in Africa. You always sleep from lunch to four o'clock.' Maybe! Perhaps the

Adventures in the African Jungle

Children of Fortune do! But, believe me, I can count on the fingers of one hand all the siestas Carl and I had during those work-filled months in Africa.

But the dinner hour is a time of true relaxation in the tropics, and it lasts a full hour, too, thank goodness. No wolfing of food then! After that, when there has been a successful hunt, all hands go to work to care for the precious specimens. Often eleven o'clock, sometimes even twelve o'clock sees the finish of that important job.

No matter what is on, you must consistently overhaul your chop boxes and see to the proper preservation of cooked food, stored away in a 'safe'—a box semi-covered with wire netting for the circulation of air and to keep out flies and other insects. And you must lock up all your supplies, or they will depart in the night—depart to the festal board of cook and tent boys. Your servants will never steal your money and seldom your clothes—but they will help themselves to sugar, butter, flour and tea, without a moral qualm, just as if you were Fortuna herself. They make no distinction, even if you are hundreds of miles away from your source of supply. They cash in on every one of the possibilities their master's store affords. It is their due, they argue—their extra *backsheesh*.

If you have had an unlucky day and no specimens are to be cared for, you can actually sit and rest for an hour before a tiny flickering camp fire, as the evening

Adventures in the African Jungle

breeze blows all about you or with a big moon casting crazy shadows among the crooked vine-clad trees. Always the time is short indeed. It is ten o'clock before you know it, and you drag your aching legs over to your tent.

You resent in yourself that acquired sense of neatness which compels you to brush your teeth and hang up your clothing properly to air—that forethought which demands that you put out your equipment for the morrow. You know Nature never intended you to be like that. You want to kick everything into a heap on your canvas floor cloth and step on it. But the relentless thought of to-morrow's job persecutes you, and you do the things you ought to do. After what seems an eternity, you crawl under your mosquito net and collapse into your little canvas bed—the most heavenly place in all this unholy world. Those filthy old hyenas may whine and laugh all they please, a hundred yards away—those jackals may yelp and bark, yes, they can even bite—that herd of zebra can trot and canter and gallop to its heart's content; that lion may talk—he may eulogize his evening meal—he may do any old thing he pleases—you don't care—you–don't-care. You—are—going—to—sleep. You—d-o-n-t—c-a-r-e—for—a-n-y-t-h-i-n-g-!

CHAPTER VIII THE REALIZATION OF A
DREAM

BY CARL AND MARY L. JOBE AKELEY

"By all the rules of the game I should have been a farmer," my husband once remarked to me. Even at a very early age he was much more interested in birds and chipmunks than in the crops and cattle on his father's farm. Taxidermy made its first appeal to him after reading a book on that subject which he borrowed from a friend. Buying books seemed needlessly extravagant at that time. From this book he acquired sufficient knowledge to justify an announcement of his new vocation. On a printed business card, he stated to the world that Carl Akeley did 'artistic taxidermy in all its branches.' To supplement his taxidermic booklore, he went so far as to take a few painting lessons from a lady in Holley, New York, a village near his home, in order that he might paint realistic backgrounds for stuffed birds and animals. So far as I know, his early attempts in this direction were the first experiments with painted backgrounds for taxidermic groups. At least one of them is still in existence, but Carl never returned to view his first efforts.

When he was nineteen, and after he had helped harvest the autumn crops, he set out to enlarge the scope of his new enterprise. In the neighboring town of Brockport lived an Englishman named David Bruce, a painter and interior decorator whose hobby was taxidermy. To the boy fresh from the farm, it seemed that Bruce lived an ideal life, because his business left him sufficient leisure for his avocation. It had not occurred to Carl then that he might ever make a living at anything so fascinating as taxidermy, and his ambition was to work with Bruce in the decorating business, in order that he might also work among the cases of stuffed birds and animals. When he called upon Bruce he found him kindly and cordial. He entertained him at dinner and gave him much friendly advice. He promised to teach the novice all the secrets of the painting and decorating trade. A glorious future seemed settled then and there for his guest.

Mr. Bruce, however, had still another suggestion to make, one which made the future seem so favorable that it almost terrified his visitor. He said he thought Carl should go to a place where taxidermy would be his real job, and told him of Ward's Natural Science Establishment, a famous institution in Rochester, which, at that time and for years afterwards, supplied the best museums of the country with collections of mounted specimens and other natural history objects. It was the headquarters of taxidermy in America.

That night Carl hardly slept a wink. He had determined upon a great venture. Early the next morning he walked three miles to the railway station to catch a train for Rochester. Traversing many of the streets of that city, his courage sinking lower and lower, he finally found a great arch made of the jaws of a sperm whale, which marked the entrance to the establishment. Once on the threshold, he was so overcome with awe that he had to walk a mile or so back and forth to summon enough courage to ring the professor's bell. Then he was ushered into an elaborately furnished room, to wait while the professor finished his breakfast. It was a long time since Carl had eaten his, and that fact seemed to increase the youth's disadvantage in the older man's presence. It was a fateful moment in Carl Akeley's career when this busy, brusque little man snapped out, "What do you want?"

Struggling to retain the last vestige of professional pride that went with the printed business card, Carl, without a word, handed him this evidence of his skill and art as a taxidermist. The bit of pasteboard seemed to have the effect of a talisman, for the great professor asked him when he could go to work, offering him the

MR. AKELEY AT THE COLOSSAL TASK OF PREPARING SINGLE HANDED
THE SKIN OF AN OLD BULL ELEPHANT FOR HIS MUSEUM GROUP.

CARL AKELEY'S GROUP, THE FIGHTING BULLS IN FIELD
MUSEUM OF NATURAL HISTORY TELL THE STORY OF
HOW ELEPHANTS CHARGE EACH OTHER IN THE
JUNGLE.

large sum of *three dollars and fifty cents a week*. Discovering a boarding house where he could get a room and meals for *four dollars a week*, Carl began to learn the art of taxidermy and to spend his slender savings.

It did not take him long to find out that his profession, chosen as the most satisfying and stimulating to his soul, was neither scientific nor artistic as then practiced at Ward's. A process was used which was simplicity itself. To mount a deer, for instance, the skin, which had been treated with salt, alum and arsenical soap, was hung upside down, the bones replaced in the legs, and the body stuffed with straw. Then, to thin the figure at any point, it was sewed through with a long needle. As can easily be imagined the creatures resulting were awkward, stilted and unnatural. There was no opportunity here to carry out Carl's dream of mounting animals in characteristic attitudes, grouped among leaves and branches, before a realistic painted background.

Carl's disappointment must have been acute when, on one occasion, he attempted to do something a little better. A zebra was brought into the establishment. Realizing that one must understand animal anatomy in order to make lifelike mountings, he had been studying bones and muscles and now he asked permission to make a plaster cast of the zebra's body. Doing it on his own time, working from supper to breakfast, and following a few original experiments in the process, he was rewarded by

[175]

having the casts thrown on the dump when morning came. The zebra was stuffed in the usual way.

Although he was not aware of it then, he understood later that crude methods were forced upon the taxidermists of that time by the fact that no one would pay for better work. Museums were interested exclusively in the collection of scientific data. They preferred bird skins to bird groups, and skeletons to mammal groups. They cared little for exhibitions that would appeal to the public. Professor Ward was forced to set a price on his work that his buyers would pay.

It was a difficult matter to combat the prevalent notion that taxidermy was of no importance and to have faith in the possibility of its development as an art. Carl was finally instrumental in obtaining for taxidermy the recognition generally accorded today. Before that happened, however, he almost deserted his chosen career to become a teacher.

William Morton Wheeler, one of his associates at Ward's, had left to teach in a high school in Milwaukee. To assist Carl in continuing an education that had early been interrupted because of lack of funds, he offered to tutor him if he would join him there. So Carl went to Milwaukee and got employment with the museum, which was to supply food and lodging while he prepared for college. It eventually did more than that, for it absorbed him so that he gave up all thought of abandoning taxidermy, and remained eight years in Milwaukee, working in the museum and in a shop of his own.

Several things happened there which stimulated his interest in his chosen work. One of the museum directors had been to Lapland, and had collected the skin of a reindeer, a sled, and the driving paraphernalia, and he was eager to have these shown in the museum. This material Carl helped assemble as a group which represented a Laplander driving a reindeer over the snow. That was fairly successful and the museum soon after was induced to buy a set of skins of orang-utans which Charles F. Adams had collected in Borneo. These, too, were arranged in a group, using some bare branches as accessories.

The reindeer and orang-utan work encouraged Carl to suggest the preparation of a series of groups of fur-bearing animals of Wisconsin. The recommendation was more tolerated than countenanced when it was first made. However while at the museum he finished a muskrat group. Just as in the case of most of his early experiments, this work was done in spite of the opposition of the authorities.

Wheeler, who was the cause both of Carl's going to Milwaukee and of his leaving it, had now become a director of the museum. While abroad in that capacity, he had talked with Sir William Flower of the British Museum, and Flower had intimated that he would like Carl to come there. So Carl planned to quit Milwaukee and go to London. However, he got no nearer than Chicago. Passing through that city, he happened into the Field Museum then housed in the old art gallery of the Columbian Exposition. It was there that Professor Daniel G. Elliot, the curator of zoology, offered him some taxidermy contracts which were accepted on the spot. While they were being carried out, Elliot suggested that Carl go with him on an expedition to Somaliland.

Thus, overcoming a thousand difficulties and obstacles, Carl Akeley, the farm boy, became a naturalist, achieving, one by one, the ambitions of his youth, until at last he stood on the threshold of the great adventure that had beckoned across the years—Africa.

With Dr. Elliot's *safari*, he plunged into Somaliland, there beginning his long journeys and his numerous experiences in the country to which he finally gave his life's devotion. His education in the field was rapid. Twice on that first expedition he stood in the shadow of death, but these experiences did not quench his thirst for adventure. On the contrary, he was never so happy as when actually in the field or when planning a new expedition. One journey succeeded another, until he became known not only as a great taxidermist and naturalist but as one of the foremost authorities on the wild life of that great continent which he chose to call 'Brightest Africa.'

Adventures in the African Jungle

In his own personal diaries, often written by the light of a flickering camp fire or a tallow candle, with the blackness of the jungle around him, Carl Akeley has recorded some of the adventures of an explorer's life on the trail. Here are stories of hunting and tracking, facts about unusual animals and strange native customs, told in the direct manner of a man who was merely jotting down the actualities of his daily existence. This journal reveals the man's love for the wild life which he sought so earnestly to protect from extermination.

Of all the animals that he encountered in his years in Africa, the elephant was perhaps the one that Carl admired and respected the most. This was true despite the fact that he was mauled and nearly killed by one of these charging beasts. No other creature seemed to him so intelligent, so courageous, or so nearly possessed of human characteristics, and nothing gave him more satisfaction than fresh discoveries about 'Tembo,' whom he always regarded as a friend rather than as an enemy.

Because his diary contains much that is interesting about the elephant and other animals, and because it gives the reader a glimpse of the hope, disappointment, labor and achievement of an explorer in the field, a part of it is included here. These notes are presented as they were set down by my husband, and they must be considered not as a story but as a series of events, recorded

[179]

Adventures in the African Jungle

as they occurred, without any attempt to confine them within the narrow limits of conventional narrative form.

*   *   *   *   *

At last I am in real elephant country and today I found a great herd. Although none of the bulls were suitable for museum specimens, I had the pleasure of watching them at short range for several hours—a pleasure that was somewhat dampened by a terrific storm.

Leaving the main trail from Mamakokola we trekked north about ten miles, and for at least half the way followed fresh tracks. Approaching the spot selected for camp, we were greeted by the squealing of the herd some distance to the right.

About noon, after maneuvering to get the wind in our favor, I saw elephants less than a half-mile away. The herd was so large that an almost continuous squealing assailed my ears. Just as I reached the rear guard, and was watching the movements of half a dozen good-sized bulls, the storm struck with tropic fury. The wind and rain made a sea of the jungle, obscuring everything. It left me more or less exposed to being accidentally 'walked on' by some restless member of the herd.

Occasionally an elephant—looking more like a wet gray wall than a living animal—loomed out of the mist. My field glasses were useless but I was close enough to observe in detail anything that penetrated the rain cur-

[180]

tain. A group of big bulls shambled past. I left the shelter of an acacia tree to examine them, but the dripping veterans were uninteresting from the standpoint of ivory. My hands were numbed by the cold and the ground was covered with three inches of water.

I started for camp, following the trail of the herd. Only then did I realize the tremendous number of elephants that must have surrounded me. The trail was from 100 to 150 feet wide and everything in that broad path had been beaten and crushed to the ground. Acacias a foot in diameter had been uprooted and thrown aside, and every trace of foliage had disappeared. It was as though a cyclone had swept the land. Reaching camp, the voices of the giants could still be plainly heard.

*   *   *   *   *

Today I saw an unusual and most interesting sight —two elephants staging a sham battle. Standing unobserved a few yards away I saw two young bulls measuring their strength in friendly combat, quite unaware of the presence of an interested and amused spectator. Playfully they charged each other, ramming their heads together in a collision that reminded me of runaway locomotives. Smash! Their wall-like skulls met with a force sufficient to knock down buildings. After each attack they faced each other, running their trunks over one another's heads—as if investigating the extent of damage—but in a friendly and most comical manner.

At length I disturbed them and the game was finished for the day. One of the players had tusks which I think must have weighed about eighty pounds each. Not an unusual weight, but fairly good for a youngster.

*   *   *   *   *

Many elephants were around camp all last night. This morning I set out to track them through the forest, little suspecting the drama the day would produce. Five hundred yards from the edge of the forest, just at the brink of a bush-filled *nullah* (gully), I climbed on an ant hill to get a 'pre-view' of the country I was about to enter. The back of an old female elephant was just visible above the grass—it was a fortunate 'look before the leap.' Soon she got my scent and moved away. I could hear no sound in the bush of the *nullah* but felt that there were more elephants there.

Moving to the top of a rocky *kopje*, some hundred yards to the left, I spotted two cows at the base of the forest side, and a fine bull at the edge of the woods. I waited on the *kopje* until *twenty-five elephants* had moved out of that little *nullah* into which I had nearly plunged so recklessly. The last of that herd, a group of seven or eight, got wind as they came out and, instead of making directly for the forest as the others had done, became confused and swung around in circles below. Their

SWIFTLY THE WHITE MAN'S RIFLES ARE EXTERMINATING
OLD TEMBO.

TWO NATIVES OF UGANDA WHOSE EARS WERE SLICED
OFF BY AN IRATE KING!

excitement increased and eventually they followed their companions into the woods.

What a picture of animation and power one gets when looking at elephants in the wild! As I stood meditating on this thought, I was suddenly aware of something happening below me in the forest. In the next few moments I received an impression that made all my previous African experiences pale into insignificance.

There was not an elephant in sight, but the forest, sloping down from higher land almost to my feet and for a mile on either side, seemed literally to boil with them. Where I stood, on top of the *kopje*, there was scarcely a breath of wind, and yet from every point of the compass came the constant crash of breaking trees. Above and through this sound penetrated the squeals and screams and roars of many hundreds of elephants. Added to this strange tumult were the hoarse calls of angry Colobus monkeys, the bark of dog-faced baboons, and the piercing, almost human, shrieks of chimpanzees.

Chills ran up and down my spine, not because of fear but because of something age-old and primitive reacting to the oldest clamor—the composite outcry of the jungle. As suddenly as it had begun, the voices of elephant and of ape were stilled. Some mysterious warning, some never-to-be-understood alarm had transfixed each beast, motionless, silent. The forest was locked in appalling stillness.

[183]

Adventures in the African Jungle

Then, while I too stood captured by the fascination of my surroundings, a great gale of wind seemed to strike the forest—yet there was not the slightest movement of air. The retreating herd, inaudible in its flight, except for the scuffling of dead leaves and the swish of branches against the bodies of hundreds of elephants, produced a sound similar to the whirring roar of a tempest. A weird and most impressive experience.

*   *   *   *   *

I have actually witnessed it! For years I have heard hunters and natives tell stories of the elephant's almost human devotion to a comrade, but until today such stories remained for me in the realm of myth.

I was in a big herd, and I saw an old fellow that seemed satisfactory for my museum group. The brush was extremely thick, but I caught a glimpse of good ivory and a gray wall of body. I followed to a little clearing, and when within fifteen yards I fired. The herd stampeded noisily and in the ensuing cloud of dust I lost sight of the big tusker for several moments. I expected a charge from the herd, but when none was forthcoming I stepped into the clearing and saw my bull had fallen about 75 feet from the spot where he had been struck.

Then came the remarkable thing. The herd had made off, but half a dozen cows detached themselves from the main body and returned to their wounded comrade.

Adventures in the African Jungle

Seeming to coöperate with great intelligence, they undertook to lift the old leader to his feet with their trunks. It was a pitiful and yet an inspiring sight. Their efforts were unavailing, but they persisted, seeming not to think of danger. They remained until the old bull was dead—a matter of a very few minutes—and then, as soon as life had unquestionably departed, they simultaneously abandoned their attempts to raise him and slowly followed the track of the herd into the forest.

The tusks of the bull will go about ninety pounds each—a good but not an extraordinary weight—but he is a remarkable beast. Height at shoulder, eleven feet four inches, and the circumference of his front foot is sixty-seven and one half inches—to my knowledge the largest that has ever been recorded.

*   *   *   *   *   *

Unexpectedly I ran on to a herd of buffalo this morning. About thirty-five of them were lying down in partly burned elephant grass. They stampeded for about a hundred yards and then turned and rushed more than half way toward me. I waited without firing, although it was an unpleasant feeling. They stood head on, ready to charge, shaking their heads and grumbling but finally they moved away. I don't think an unwounded buffalo will attack, but his manner at times is most disconcerting.

Later, when returning to camp, I heard elephants and

Adventures in the African Jungle

climbed an ant hill to look them over. The tall grass where they were feeding was shaking and swaying, but I could not get a good view until they emerged on a stretch of high ground fifty yards away. There were eleven, all cows and young animals. Thinking a bull might follow, I waited, but the wind had shifted and was blowing toward the animals. Then came the long-drawn rumble, like distant thunder, which announces a charge. This was followed immediately by the indescribable bellowing screams of infuriated elephants. They came on a hundred yards and stopped. I prayed that the charge was over but they had only lost scent for a moment. In another second they had located me and the entire herd, backing the leader, came at full speed.

Ears and trunks flying like torn sails and broken masts in a storm at sea, they bore down upon me, screaming horribly until it seemed as if nothing could stop them. Someone was going to be hurt. David Harum's motto—"Be sure, and do it first"—seemed to fit the circumstances. My first shot stopped the leader but she recovered almost instantly and, with the others at her back, renewed the assault. The next bullet brought her down and discouraged her followers. Fortunately they turned and started off. They were much too close for my comfort and I was in no position to meet a further attack.

It seems to me that the elephant's ability to follow a scent so accurately, combined with the disposition—on the part of the cows at least—to charge when they smell man, is sufficient to put them at the head of the list of dangerous game.

En route through the forest, I passed three *shambas* that were completely devastated. Not a banana tree left standing nor a potato in the ground. Just the remnants of the huts, and groups of disconsolate natives. When hungry elephants actually get into a *shamba* the natives are absolutely helpless, and any outcry from the huts is likely to result in a charge bringing destruction to the dwellings and death to their inhabitants. Once Tembo acquires a taste for bananas and sweet potatoes, the native gardener may just as well look for a new home.

* * * * * *

I passed through three deserted villages today, during a hot four-and-a-half-hour march. Probably the villages were not raided by elephants until the inhabitants had left. In the largest one, indications of hurried departure were unmistakable. Even food and household utensils had been abandoned. Evidently the people left in a panic—perhaps after sleeping sickness had killed many of them. I have been badly bitten by various insects, but I have not seen the tsetse-fly—at least I have not recognized it.

* * * * *

Adventures in the African Jungle

The chief local guide of the region came into camp and reported that he had found the trail of a good bull elephant. Deciding to have a look, I started at six this morning, and an hour later found a fresh trail. Later I located seven bulls—the same lot I spotted a week ago —loafing about a water hole. I took some photos and returned to camp at noon. It is easy to hear or 'feel' the roar of Murchison Falls as I sit here in camp.

Today's four-hour march led over a range of hills. They are clothed in bamboo, the first I have seen in Uganda. It is a bamboo that is perfectly solid, growing in big clumps. After a stiff climb to the top of a hill, I stopped to have a look for game. Almost immediately, I noticed a herd of fifty or more elephants two miles away. A little later we discovered another herd—perhaps one hundred and fifty members—ranging directly in the line of march. I had lunched at this vantage point, eating while keeping an eye on the game. The first herd began to work nearer and I set out as it disappeared into the forest at the base of the hills.

Half way to the bottom, a number of buffalo crossed the trail and delayed the descent. The elephants were in a grass patch beyond a line of bush and the wind would not allow keeping up above them. Following the buffalo across a stream and up onto a ridge, I had a good view of the herd—all cows and small animals.

* * * * *

Adventures in the African Jungle

Porters came in late yesterday with the skin and skull of a bull I shot near the Nile. The tusks weighed 76 and 80 pounds respectively. I paid off twenty-two of the porters and took care of the skin. Yesterday a telegram came asking if I had been killed, as no word had been received from me at Nairobi.

* * * * *

Made an early start and took up the trail of a large herd. Met several small bands, but they got wind and scattered each time. Finally, at the end of a ravine, Bill spotted a nice pair of tusks, but we could see little of the beast's head. I could hardly see the sights of my gun but, as the big fellow began to move away, I took hurried aim and let go both barrels. Almost echoing the shots, we heard the elephant fall with a mighty crash. He got up, however, and we followed, his trail being quite plain. Suddenly the fearful noise of a tree being torn up by the roots informed us of his presence on our left, and with a roar he charged. His aim was poor and, crossing twenty feet in front of us, I was enabled to finish him with two bullets.

It was a beautiful pair of symmetrical tusks. One weighed 102 pounds and measured twenty-one and one-half inches in circumference at the skull. We began the work of skinning him at once.

* * * * *

Adventures in the African Jungle

Finished the skin preparation in these past three days, under pleasant conditions in camp, in the great forest of buttressed trees. The chimpanzees furnish amusement but sometimes they become a nuisance. Either they resent our being here or else, monkey-like, they have nothing better to do than attempt to annoy us. Every once in a while we receive a shower of dead limbs and sticks, accompanied by a scolding chatter, to remind us of their presence. Occasionally their aim is too good not to suggest deliberate malice. The ticks are with us too.

*   *   *   *   *

It was raining hard at daybreak and looked like a day of it, so I decided to take it easy, but the boys found the trail where a bull had crossed into the forest and, taking Bill, I followed it. The bull led us a long chase, but the weather was clearing so we kept on. In a dense forest we met a troop of chimpanzees making a frightful row. Apparently the 'chimps' were on the ground, but they kept ahead of us continually demonstrating their vocal ability. Suddenly there was a new note to the chorus—a voice so deep and strong that I could not help but believe it to be a gorilla. The shouting and screaming was accompanied by distant drumming. It did not sound like chest-beating but exactly like the rapid beating of a log drum with two sticks.

My thoughts were on the chimpanzees when suddenly

there was a grand stampede of the guides. They took positions behind me, and then I saw the old bull we had been trailing crashing through the bush ahead of us. He gave the charge scream and started for us but ended his rush midway. It looked—and sounded—like the real thing, but proved to be another anti-climax when he turned and made off through the forest.

We followed for two hours, until we came to a 'rubber road' in the forest, which led toward camp and which I told the boys to follow. Bill and I climbed a rocky ledge, made tea and had a belated lunch. Nothing of interest in the afternoon, and we returned to camp. We were nearly smothered by flies at dark and had our supper under a net. Probably not the sleeping-sickness fly, as they were not 'scissor wings,' but they bit viciously just the same.

*   *   *   *   *

Bill and I made a leisurely start this morning. I laid out a general course from camp—north and then west —circling a hill in the forest and keeping to heavy timber where we had been hearing chimpanzees and elephants. After being in the forest for an hour or so, we stopped to photograph a buttressed tree and soon heard chimpanzees making a great noise. We had no difficulty getting close to them as they were in the tree tops, and we had a good view of perhaps a dozen individ-

[191]

Adventures in the African Jungle

uals. I made some photos, but as soon as they discovered our presence they did their best to frighten us away with terrifying screams and roars. They made feints of attacking us, and we had constantly to be on the lookout for falling deadwood. An old male wrenched off a large green limb, carried it across the tree tops and launched it at Bill, missing him only by inches.

An hour later we heard a swish of branches and attributed it to monkeys, but soon discovered our mistake. We were in a big elephant herd and its members seemed to be in a bad temper. Our position was delicate, as the wind was from the *safari* to the herd, and if I got on the other side they might turn and charge the boys. I began the stalk hoping to move the *safari* out of range of a possible attack, but the elephants had scented me and were talking in a nasty manner.

One old cow threatened continually to charge—she had a very young *toto* with her. I avoided her, and the herd moved off slowly and in an obviously dangerous mood. I saw no unusual specimens and no particularly good ivory.

*　　*　　*　　*　　*

We marched an hour or so toward Masindi and camped. The baboons were extremely numerous. They came into the *shamba*, where we had placed our tents, and met us face to face, and I couldn't hurt them. They are very bold and show no signs of fear.

*   *   *   *   *

Went out to shoot kongoni for food. This is a flat country with grass more than three feet high. The ground is pitted with elephant tracks, made during the rainy season, which are now like small jagged craters. Very rough going. I got two kongoni and one bull elephant.

*   *   *   *   *

Today I came to the place that had been my camping ground eight months ago. The steward in charge here has no ears. When he was a boy, he once looked at a king; but native boys do not enjoy the privilege proverbially accorded cats. The jungle ruler, angered at the youth's boldness, had his ears cut off. One of our porters suffered a somewhat similar fate many years ago when a prisoner of the Waganda. His tormentors contented themselves with slicing away one ear. I photographed the steward and the porter together.

The old days of torture and brutality are about ended, but occasionally I encounter some evidence of what conditions were when local chieftains held unlimited power. Recently I heard of an old fellow who, though quite respectable nowadays, was something of a

[193]

Adventures in the African Jungle

terror in his youth. Upon coming of age, and to demonstrate his manhood to the elders of the tribe, he cut up a prisoner alive. Starting with ankles and wrists he continued his savage butchery until his victim was carved into a hundred pieces.

* * * * *

CHAPTER IX · CHAKULA

BY MARY L. JOBE AKELEY

Tum, tum, tum, tum, tum-m-m-m-m-m;

Tum, tum, tum, tum, tum-m-m-m-m-m.

THE old 'granddaddy' spoon is making an awful racket with the big, black frying pan. *"Chakula! Chakula!"* "First, last and only call to lunch!" "Come a' running!" "Come and get it!" or even "Lunch is served." That is what your cook means when he calls *"Chakula!"* No matter what he might say if he spoke English you know that his *chakula* (food) is ready and if you want to keep peace in the sacred quarters of the kitchen, you will drop your work on the instant, wash up quickly and start in the direction whence is coming the melodious voice. *"Ndiyo mpishi,* (Yes, cook)" you call, as you step out lively to the dining tent.

The cook's *kelele* (noise) is by no means an unwelcome sound. In fact it is just the sound you are longing to hear. It was in the early pre-dawn that you had your

[195]

Adventures in the African Jungle

first cup of tea, and just before sun-up you ate the conventional breakfast of stewed fruit, porridge—no, you never eat porridge anywhere—but the others did—bacon, toast and coffee. Now, a full hour ago the sun slid across the meridian and at one o'clock it is time for all the world to take a little rest. Hot? It *is* hot. Everywhere in Equatorial Africa, except up in the nine or ten thousand foot altitudes, it is undeniably hot at noon. In some places the heat is really sickening—for example, at the coast or in the low altitudes of two thousand feet or less in the interior valleys. And even when we camped at five to six thousand feet above sea level, in the Central African plateau, we all freely admitted that it was hot enough to take a full hour off for lunch. This we were able to do when on location in our base camps.

At noon in the highlands of Kenya the Fahrenheit thermometer usually registered about seventy-eight to eighty degrees—sometimes it would go as high as eighty-five in the shade. And there was no use to deny it, the sun blazed on from eleven until three. But there was almost always a fresh breeze and when under canvas we had much to be thankful for. We were not forced to endure the sweltering heat that radiates from high stone buildings or from cement pavements. Each night the winds from snow-capped Kenya and Kilimanjaro submerged all the land in coolness and refreshed it and all that slept therein. Heavy dews evaporated throughout the morning. Under the high overhanging boulders the shade continued deep and cool—as the 'shadow of a great rock in a weary land.'

During the early hours of the day, there was much comfort in our green canvas tents, each with its fly raised more than a foot above the top. As my tent was large enough to move about a little in it, I could shift my work table easily as the sun rose high. Outstretched above me, too, I had a royal red canopy of heavy, sun-proof felt. It was actually a remnant of the large marquee the English King had used on his last Dunbar in India. I had been a bit fascinated by the brilliant stuff when I had seen it in the big warehouse of our London outfitters; and Carl, unknown to me, had told them to ship it with our other dunnage. With his accustomed thoughtfulness, he had sensed what a comfort it would be to me on this, my first trip to the tropics. Finally, near the end of our year's *safari*, little Bob, my ten-year-old Baganda *toto*, appropriated it as his 'blanketty' (blanket) and refused to be separated from it thereafter.

But even with such a regal awning for my protection, it required real effort to stick at a mental job until noon. As a matter of fact, the first week I was in Africa I had gotten a small 'dose of sun' by riding in a motor while the sun hit my back. My head had been well protected by my sun helmet, but then I had not realized that it is equally essential always to protect the spine.

Adventures in the African Jungle

This 'sun dose' stayed with me for over six weeks. It seemed that my spine became red hot each day as noon approached, and I had a little fever as well. So much will power was thus necessary for my work that the cook's *"Chakula!"* was usually a grateful sound.

Do you wonder what we had for lunch on the average day? The meal usually began by filling our big white drinking cups with water—cooled by evaporation in our large canvas water coolers. To this, we added unsweetened Rose's lime juice—a very boon in the tropics, where raw products are seldom obtainable, and an excellent substitute for fresh citrus fruits. To my mind, unsweetened lime juice has a great advantage over the sweetened variety, because it is far more thirst quenching and you can always add sugar should you crave a sweet drink.

Drinking water is always boiled. Depraved indeed is any servant who neglects the proper boiling of water. He knows this is an absolute necessity for the white man. You would think so too if you could see the streams and pools from which our supply is often obtained. Water is not abundant in Africa. This is not due especially to light rainfall but rather to the fact that there are 'long rains' and 'short rains' with long periods of drought in between. Still more important is the character of the soil, which is porous. Therefore, the rainfall is seldom retained in clay pockets such as form the perpetual springs and sources of life-giving streams in

Adventures in the African Jungle

many sections of our own country. Then, too, in almost every part of Equatorial Africa, innumerable natives, throughout countless centuries, have gradually cut down the primeval forests. Thus the natives have prevented the conservation of their richest possession—an abundant water supply.

The drinking water is usually boiled in the late afternoon. In fact, if you are on the march, the cook sees to it the moment his evening fire is made. Eight or ten porters are sent to the water hole or stream. Soon they appear marching along in single file, each with a 'debbie' of water on his head. Quickly your thirty-gallon water tanks are filled—one for the cook and one for the rest of the camp.

Nearly all water must be settled. Then it must be cooled before drinking. The settling is done by stirring into the boiling water a small quantity of powdered alum. Within a very few minutes all the sediment, vegetable matter, mud—whatever it may be—falls to the bottom, and you can pour the clear water off the top. Then, you fill the large canvas water coolers, cylindrical containers about twenty-four inches in length and eight inches in diameter and with a faucet at the bottom.

This water cooler is now hung in the shade of tree or tent, where the air can circulate freely around it. The canvas soon becomes water soaked; evaporation sets in, and the temperature of the water speedily goes down. By morning the water is delightfully cool, because often the night temperature has fallen to sixty-five degrees. This is now the time to fill your own individual water bottles. You must soak their canvas covers thoroughly, to cause evaporation, and thereby maintain the coolness of your draught.

As I have said, the question of sufficient or desirable water is often a serious one. There are comparatively few rivers, lakes and swamps in Equatorial Africa. In the dry season, the streams are small and often polluted; in the rainy season, they overflow with murky silt-laden waters. Many streams are by nature so strongly alkaline that it is dangerous to drink the water without filtering.

The most potent and undesirable waters I found in Africa were in and about Lake Hannington. I was anxious to see this wildly beautiful lake in the Great Rift Valley and I had my husband's unfinished task to accomplish there. This lake was named in honor of a great adventurer, James Hannington, who in 1885 was so eager to explore a new route to Uganda that he dared enter the territory of a hostile native king, Mwanga, who murdered him and all his followers. "I have purchased the road to Uganda with my blood," the explorer cried, as the native spears impaled him on either side. And so I found, as an adventurer of today whose work required a visit to this great sheet of water with its shifting 'islands' of pink flamingoes, that the hostile, volcanic rocks demand their toll of blood of one who would gain the sources of the lake. These are full flowing streams of hot alkaline water, unfit to drink even when cooled.

On the brink of the lake are large boiling springs, gushing forth from volcanic depths, and whose clouds of steam are visible many miles away. On closer approach you find a wide area of alkaline deposit encrusting the ground round about. Take a peek at the greenish-blue depths, and you draw back quickly, lest you be overcome by the powerful fumes or get in the path of a heavy steam jet. Standing in the fetid waters of the lake and along its shores, are dead trees—the remains of an ancient forest. Now they serve as perches and nesting places for storks, herons and eagles. Near all this abundance of water there is little green vegetation. The high alkalinity of the water, the subterranean fires —all make of this great valley a wild desolation.

Once in a long while in Africa you find a spring of sweet, clear and abundant water. There is one such at the camp of the white hunter, A. J. Klein, in Tanganyika, and to this we sent our motor lorries, when they could be spared, a distance of sixty miles each way, with our tanks to be filled with drinking water. Otherwise we drew from the same water holes as supplied His Majesty, the Lion. Other *safaris* have carried the pure waters of the Klein spring a much greater distance. This fountain head quenches the thirst of many natives who

Adventures in the African Jungle

graze their flocks on the outlying meadows. It irrigates the large vegetable garden from which Klein so generously supplies his friends who camp near by. In this locality it is one of nature's greatest gifts widely known and universally blessed.

We camped by another such spring, one day's march southwest of Rutshuru on the trail to the Gorilla Sanctuary in the Belgian Congo. It supplies an even larger number of natives than does the Klein spring, and also the *shamba* of a white settler. But I have never seen in Africa such spring brooks as are found in our own meadows and forests, or such swift running streams as ripple among our hills and valleys. Only in the higher reaches of Africa's snow-capped mountains did I find anything even remotely resembling the sweet waters I had taken for granted since childhood.

Therefore, when you go to Africa you must be content to have any kind of water at all—in fact you should be thankful. Try not to crave or even remember the bubbling springs and rills of the homeland. Be deeply grateful for the rain water you find in the large galvanized iron tanks attached to the roofs of almost every dwelling, and offer up an oblation to the gods if ever, in the dense shade of wild fig trees or in some abrupt mountain wall, you chance upon a spring of sweet and cold and sparkling water. If once you are so lucky, you will certainly drink to home and country.

Adventures in the African Jungle

But our luncheon is not limited to liquid refreshment. Soon the main dish appears in the form of a large bowl of steaming rice—cooked as only African natives or East Indians can cook it. Each grain is soft, dry and separate —not at all resembling the gelatinous mass we are so often compelled to eat in the homeland. Of course, you buy the unpolished rice or the wild brown rice when you can get it. It is rubbed hard in the washing in order to remove every particle of adhering flour. Next it is put over the fire in cold water and allowed to boil vigorously without a cover. When tender it is drained, washed in cold water and set in a colander to dry over or near the fire. The native cooks in Africa spoil you completely for eating rice prepared by anyone else.

With the rice, your boy serves the curry. Curry powder or paste is a well-known Oriental condiment, the name being derived from the Tamil *kari*, a sauce or relish for rice. It consists of an elaborate mixture of many Eastern spices and the leaves of the curry-leaf tree. No matter how small a portion of meat, fowl, or game has been left from last night's dinner, your cook optimistically informs you, "Plenty for curry."

Freshly ground curry powder may be purchased when in a town, in almost any Indian bazaar. The cook now adds this pungent flavoring to a rich and abundant sauce made of butter, flour, and a little tinned cream, with a dash of vinegar. To this sauce the bits of cooked meat have been added. Sometimes when there is no meat left over, the cook uses hard boiled eggs. You can obtain fresh eggs almost everywhere from the natives.

Sometimes your cook boils raisins with the rice. In any event an appetizing Major Gray's India chutney (Hindustani *chatni*) is always served with curry and rice. It is a spicy pickle of sweet fruits, such as mangoes, raisins and apple. It is flavored with acid tamarinds, lemons, limes and sour herbs and with hot seasoning of chili, cayenne pepper and other spices. Strange as it may seem, men who live in low latitudes or 'under the sun' invariably crave highly seasoned food.

I cared little for curry and rice and chutney in the beginning, but it soon grew to be a staple luncheon dish of which we seldom tired. My own portion of curry was prepared with lighter seasoning, because the full-strength condiment which the men of our expedition so generally enjoyed was too high powered for my palate.

Alternating with curry and rice, on our menu were baked dishes, such as macaroni and cheese, tomatoes or escalloped potatoes. Then we had tinned succotash, green lima beans, peas, or some other ordinary vegetable, just as you have on camping trips at home. These vegetables accompanied cold boiled ham, a very real delicacy, or cold cuts of fresh meat. Following this, usually came our most popular dessert, tinned fruit. Tea was brought to us at four-thirty, while we worked; but at that hour of the day it was just plain tea, without cake or biscuits.

When in permanent camp in the field our dinner was at seven, but it was served later when in the town. It was any time between six-thirty and nine when on motor *safari*, depending upon how far we chose or were compelled to travel in order to find a camp site with wood and water. Our dinners varied, according to how much time the cook had to prepare his meal. But he generally surprised us with more rather than with less, and a good cook will boil and bake and stew long after dark in his effort to have a pleasing menu for the following day. When on the march, certain cooked foods, prepared the night before, are carried in *safari* pots and sometimes in a most casual and improvised manner. Often it is best for you to know little or nothing about your cook's management of these details. There is little doubt but that one gets his full 'peck of dirt' when on an African *safari*.

While in permanent camp, and not too far from native gardens, the variety and appetizing quality of the evening meal is often astonishing. You always have soup, a roast of meat or fowl, with proper 'white man's potatoes' and sometimes the native sweet potato or yam, which is the only potato your black boys will eat. You may even have green string beans, peas, squash, or young and tender native corn. Almost always you can buy bananas from the natives, because they are one of their staple foods.

When in a town like Nairobi or Kampala, you may have, in addition, carrots, green onions, beets, okra and cabbage, raised in the Indian gardens. As long as possible, you carry on *safari* a supply of the less perishable fresh vegetables, which you have carefully purchased in the market. There, too, you can frequently buy oranges, limes, guavas, lemons, pineapples and papayas. Growing abundantly in every white man's garden, the papaya is a delicious fruit, oblong and yellow, and has a pulpy flesh like a melon and thick rind with a hollow enclosing numerous black seeds.

In our own garden in our Nairobi base we had an unusual supply of all these tropic fruits and many vegetables. For *safari* you pack the least perishable fruits and vegetables in large open-meshed native baskets, for the free circulation of air, which is the best of nature's preservatives in the tropics. You can always carry without difficulty, over a period of several weeks, both white potatoes and ripened onions.

When your luxuries of fresh fruit and green vegetables are exhausted, you must turn to your English chop (food) boxes, carefully prepared in the Army and Navy Stores in London, and replenished from one of the excellent English markets in the town. These con-

Photo. by Mary L. Jobe Akeley.

MWANIKA BAKED EXCELLENT BREAD IN A
NATURAL ROCK OVEN.

MRS. AKELEY'S PRIZE COOK, HIS HELPERS AND HIS
KITCHEN IN THE LUKENIA HILLS.

THE WAKAMBA BRING IN THEIR CHICKENS AND EGGS
TO SELL IN THE WHITE MAN'S CAMP.

Adventures in the African Jungle

tain all tinned goods, sugar, flour, sauces and biscuits. Soon you become tired of game and fowl, because they lack in fat and therefore are of poor flavor. As a real delicacy you may have a special viand, such as tinned corned beef hash or smoked tongue or tinned 'bully beef.' It is surprising how you crave smoked meat in the tropics. Pickles and green and ripe olives brighten the menu. Cheese, jam, biscuits and coffee close the meal, unless the cook has insisted on making one of his English steamed puddings with custard sauce, which he does very well indeed and which he will give you three or four times a week if left to his own devices.

Many times I baked apple pie—good old-fashioned American apple pie—made of tinned apple sauce prepared by an American packer. By doing so I 'achieved great merit' with the men of our expedition. I am almost ashamed to admit it, but several times I experimented with lemon meringue pie. Just imagine baking a meringue pie in the African jungle! It gave an hour of much ill-concealed merriment to the cook and to all the boys when *Memsahib* baked the pie crust and then cooked the lemon custard in a double boiler. They bit their lips and their ears twitched while within range of my eyes, and I felt sure they were grinning openly behind my back. Then came the baking of the filling in the crust itself, and the final exciting moment when the beaten up whites of the eggs became the finished meringue. My cook assisted me most conscientiously in the baking, caring for the oven by adding or raking off a few embers here and there with all the concern of the proper servant. Often the meringue turned out a most delectable light brown, but sometimes, when the oven was too hot, it demanded definite apologies. However, it was always eaten; and that, after all, was the 'proof of the lemon pie.'

Two of my cooks made remarkably good bread. A third one made something he called bread, but the less remembered about its taste the better. For the baking of bread, the African cooks use a very simple oven. It is just a heavy reinforced sheet-iron pan, about eighteen to twenty inches square, and about six inches deep, with an inch of overlap. After the fire burns down into a bed of red-hot coals, and the oven has been allowed to become thoroughly heated, the loaves of properly leavened bread are put in. Then the oven is set well down among the glowing ashes and the top is covered thickly with embers.

For an hour the cook is unrelaxing in his vigilance. He takes his task more than seriously. At frequent intervals, he cautiously lifts up one corner of the cover and peeps in to see if all is well. If so, he closes the oven quickly with a satisfied grin. If something is going wrong, you know it, even though you may not understand his freely spoken imprecations. His tone and his expression are in themselves the key to his inner feelings. If the baking is not proceeding as he wishes, he packs on more embers and shouts to the kitchen *toto* to build up the fire near by and be quick about it. But if, as is more likely, his fire is too strong, and the bread has begun to burn before rising properly, he rakes off the embers in a very frenzy of haste and sets his oven in a smaller bed of coals.

For lifting the hot base of the oven, he uses a big gunny sack, but he does not hesitate to brush the embers off the top with his naked hand. Many a time I have seen my black boys pick up red-hot coals and leisurely light their pipes and cigarettes. I have seen them stand barefoot in hot ashes that would instantly blister the feet of a white man. And when a torch or warmth was needed, I have seen my Congo boys carry for a considerable distance a firebrand charred and burning almost in its entirety, using only their naked hands.

If for any reason the cook's oven fails—if it burns out, or is broken in transport—he is by no means 'up against it.' He is resource itself. In every motor *safari,* petrol (gasolene) is carried in large five gallon tins. These tins, when empty, have a thousand uses. I have seen two of them placed side by side and converted into an oven for the baking of six fine loaves of bread. The fire was managed in just the same way as for the regular oven, and a flattened-out part of another petrol tin was used as a covering for the open ends. Among the natives there is certainly no lack of invention.

Once my cook built his baking fire on the ground under a dome-shaped hollow rock. There was a small opening just large enough to receive his pans. He had raked out the burning brands and had leveled off the embers. Here was an oven fit for the prince of all cooks. And what sweet, nut-brown bread was baked in its steady heat! It was a sad day for all of us when Mwanika's superheated rock-oven blew up into fragments, dusting the loaves with ashes and scattering them about the landscape.

Once the cook finishes his bread baking, he carefully glosses the loaves over with butter and places them on a board or chop box to cool. During the cooling process, the cook receives many a compliment from passing white man or black—which latter dearly covets this delicacy from his master's table. Later, the cook wraps the loaves in a piece of clean 'Americani,' and puts them in a tin box to prevent their drying out. More than once, I have been called by my cook to come to his kitchen and look at his successful baking; often he has carried an exceptionally fine loaf down to my tent to show me his achievement. You can certainly forgive such a cook his boastfulness, because nowhere else in all the world is bread more essentially the staff of life.

The cooks secure their yeast in some mysterious way.

Adventures in the African Jungle

It is often passed on from one cook to another like a tradition. A proper cook always knows where to go in the town for good live yeast, and he treasures this leaven as the vestal virgins guarded their fires in temples of old.

Of course, there are many times when you are so far from a base of supplies that even with a fair cook your menus become insufferably dull—when your food reeks of the alkali water in which it has been cooked, or when a sand storm whirls its way into every pot and pan and coats every one of your dishes nicely laid out on a clean table cloth. Then you feed on grit—or else forego it. In a forlorn moment you recall the feelings of Mark Twain which he portrayed in 'A Tramp Abroad,' one of the delightful books of your childhood. You remember the 'good things' he promised himself when his journeyings were finished and he should set foot on native soil. You are 'jolly well sure' you will have some 'good things', too, once you reach home. You can see his 'suggested dishes' as he arranged them on the printed page.

American coffee with real cream
Porterhouse steak
Fried chicken, Southern style
Brook trout from the Sierra Nevada
Lake trout from Tahoe
Black bass from the Mississippi

Adventures in the African Jungle

American roast beef

Roast turkey, Thanksgiving style, cranberry sauce, celery

Canvas back duck from Baltimore

Prairie hens from Illinois

'Possum, coon

Boston bacon and beans

Bacon and greens, Southern style

Oh, well! You brush the sand off your corner of the cloth. You open a tin of sardines and quickly slip two of them in between hard sea biscuits slyly extracted from the big tin box. Your companions do likewise. It works pretty well. You all munch sardines and biscuits. You drink cautiously out of your water bottle—refraining from using the gritty cup. The boys and the cook can have the sandy food you refuse to eat. Then you open individual tins of pineapple, and each man goes at it—straight from tin to mouth—and most of the sand is missed. "Oh, well! We're in Africa," we all agree cheerfully when the 'inner man' has stopped complaining, "and we wouldn't change places with anyone else in all the world."

Sometimes in cases of emergency you have had to go on slim rations—occasionally you have gone without. In some weak moment you have positively longed for sparkling glass and silver and for all the graces of a civilized table; time and again you have wished for just the plain, old-fashioned cooking of the negro 'mammy' of your childhood. But no matter what your feelings may have been, even about the worst food you have been compelled to eat, rest assured that once you are back in the city's roar, and have become a part of the great multitude, you will find yourself wishing again in a not-too-far-distant day for your little green linen tents in Africa. You will long for that strange mixture of primitive sights and sounds and scents that are part and parcel of an African camp. Your nostrils will crave the sweet and penetrating fragrance of your *mpishi's* smoky cook-fire. And finally you will yearn past all belief for the dog-like contentment of the star-lit hour that follows a dinner of your cook's best—a dinner of pungent and strangely cooked *chakula*.

CHAPTER X   RHINOCEROS

BY CARL AKELEY

You're a tenderfoot in Africa and there's a row in the jungle! Some huge, violent beast is plunging about in the thick thorn bush. You cannot see him. So he has all the terrors of the unknown. Your heart jumps right up into your throat. You think a quick S.O.S. prayer. Suddenly you glimpse a huge lead-colored bulk cutting circles in the wild landscape. Did you ever see a pig try to play? He is the most awkward thing on earth—except a rhinoceros. Now a long, sabre-like horn is ripping around in the foliage. Grunt! Snort! Grunt! Snort! Swish! Swosh! He is off and back in a thunderhead of dirt and dust and noise. All the lesser jungle folk rush to cover. Old Father Rhino is having one of his frequent fits of bad temper. Or it may even be Mother Rhino—the old vixen! Her temper is just as touchy and uncertain as her spouse's. They just cannot bear themselves nor any other living thing. They have a bad reputation. Look

[214]

Adventures in the African Jungle

out! He's coming! The bushes crash. A face that looks like all the devils at once comes rushing in your direction. You gulp down that unruly heart that clogs your throat. Someone who knows all about rhinos fires a shot. It ploughs up the sand in front of the animal's face and covers him with a screen of dirt and dust. He swerves and vanishes in the jungle, or else stops stone still in his tracks. In any case, you breathe again and think 'your life is saved.' Now, let us see whether you are right or wrong.

Big game hunters have one favorite pastime. They love to argue about which are the most dangerous of African wild animals. Almost invariably they place the rhinoceros—or rhino, as he is known everywhere in Africa, somewhere near the top of the list. But does he belong there? He is, I admit, a formidable beast, a living threat of death or danger. But it is safe to say that very few of these hunters have waited to see what would happen if they did not meet a rhino's charge with a volley of rifle bullets. It would take a lot more than curiosity, even scientific curiosity, regarding a rhino's habits and character, to keep a man, who is in his right mind, from shooting when one of these ungainly creatures of unusual size and fierce aspect makes a rush in his direction.

The rhino wears the grouchiest expression of any of the jungle beasts. The lion's hostility is fiercely swift,

Adventures in the African Jungle

but it is dignified and usually reluctant. The buffalo is treacherous, vindictive and vengeful. The elephant is crafty, sudden, direct and purposeful. But the rhino just goes crazy drunk and runs amok. The lines of his jaw suggest determination, which he does not possess. His sharply pointed ears cock belligerently, and two horny spikes surmount his nose at such an angle that you often wonder how it would feel to be impaled on the longest and sharpest of them or tossed from them to whirl through space. Moreover, whenever the rhino catches the scent of man, he starts to charge about, often in aimless uncertainty. Because his manner is so terrifying, he has succeeded in getting himself shot up, just as he has established for himself a reputation for ferocity. Since he is a 'bad actor' you are always on the lookout for him.

I had hunted in Africa for some months when something happened to change my idea of the rhino. It prevented me from accepting the traditional view of the beast and shooting to save myself every time one got wind of me and came snorting and puffing in my direction.

I was caught unarmed by an old rascal one day on the high banks of the Tana. The animal came charging through the bushes toward me, and I had no weapon but a camera at hand. Twenty-five feet of open ground separated me from the scrubby forest through which he was plowing. There was nothing within reach to climb. He could travel much faster than I could. He would speedily run me down if I attempted to escape from him. My only hope for safety was to lie in an overhanging bush, growing over the brink of a cliff that made a sheer drop to the crocodile-infested river thirty feet below. The bush might or might not hold my weight, but I determined to swing out on it. I trusted that the rhino would rush past me into the river and that by some lucky chance I would not join him there.

The bushes parted and crashed down. The rhino plunged headlong into the open where, for the first time, he could see me. Trembling, I jumped backward toward my bush. Then the unexpected happened. The rhino stopped short, drooped his head and almost closed his small pig-like eyes. His whole attitude indicated that he was going to sleep. He ignored my presence so completely that only my sense of humor kept me from making some reply to his insult. By this time my gun boy was aware that my camera studies had been interrupted. He poked me in the back with my gun, but I had no heart to shoot the great dozing hulk before me. A more stupid, more harmless, more ludicrous object I had never beheld.

With my gun half aimed, I talked to him, to rouse him from his doze, but he stood there motionless, refusing to notice me, until my *safari*, coming through the bushes, provoked another charge. I could hear the thump-thump of the loads dropping to the ground as the black boys took to the trees or dashed out of his way, but he drove aimlessly through them and then sauntered off into the bush. The stage had been set for a tragedy but the play proved to be a farce.

After you have discovered that the rhino is the greatest bluffer in all Africa, you will find that the old chap furnishes most of the comedy for the drama of the jungle. His bluff succeeds because of his sinister aspect, rather than because he executes any cunningly contrived plan. If by accident you once get close enough to him to study his appearance, you will soon see that he really looks more stolid and dull than dangerous. His narrowing forehead rises in a peak that would resemble a dunce-cap if its outline were not broken by his perky ears. His shoe-button eyes seem sewed on at the wrong place. Folds of thick, wrinkled hide nearly bury them, and his two horns are always in the way when he wants to look directly in front of him.

Should a rhino happen to run over you, that would be dangerous of course. It would probably also be fatal. But I am convinced that the rhino is much too logy to have an accurate objective or a fixed purpose, and that, if he does run you down, it is a chance happening. I do not argue from a single instance, but rather from a long list of close-up encounters, when I insist that the rhino's

Adventures in the African Jungle

claim to be one of the four most dangerous African animals is all a bluff and that in reality he is as stupid as the elephant is wise.

Rhinos have bad eyesight. Their range of vision is probably not over fifty or sixty yards. In addition to the great horns on his nose blurring the target of his charge, he is extremely near-sighted. He probably sees 'men as trees walking,' only vague shadows at twenty or thirty paces. Therefore, when a pair of horns breaks the line of vision of a pair of half blind eyes, an angry and excited rhino literally does not know where he is going. Under such handicaps he starts a charge, and unless the wind enables him to follow scent, his charge usually develops into a ludicrous display of aimless anger. But when these absurd charges do chance to be driven home, look out! A rhino would probably attack a mountain or an ant hill if he did not happen to like the smell of it. And when the object of his random assault is large enough, he may hit it.

A friend of mine was on a train on the Uganda Railway when a resentful old rhino, probably smelling it, set out on his customary charge. The train was standing still in the middle of the plain when the occupants of the car were brought to the platform by a terrific jolt. The rhino, rushing ahead at full speed, had crashed into one of the coaches. The impact knocked him down, but he scrambled to his feet and trotted off a bit groggily, apparently satisfied that railway trains were not to be routed by such a method.

Victor Forbin, writing in the Parisian magazine, *La Nature*, tells us that another train on the same railway was actually derailed by a rhino's furious onset. It was night. The lights of the train, its dim bulk, its rush along the rails, deeply insulted a strolling rhino. He promptly attacked at a furious gallop. Biff! He knocked loose from the locomotive a steel plate, which dropped beneath a wheel, and the rhino's puffing enemy was at once derailed. But the beast had made one charge too many and lay beside the track completely 'knocked out.'

But even rhinos, reckless though they are, may fall into a panic and bolt as blindly as they attack. A few years ago a hunter's camp was invaded one moonlit night by a group of rhinos. The campers were in terror, dreading that the animals would charge their scent in a moment more. But before the great beasts could destroy either tents or occupants, one blundering rhino upset a plank on which the kitchen utensils had been stored. The terrible clatter of plates, cups, pans and kettles was a new noise to him, and more than he could stand; so off they all lumbered in a headlong panic of flight.

The rhino's clothes are much too large for him. His skin does not fit. It lies loosely draped upon his massive frame and gathers up in great folds and wrinkles. These overlapping creases form ideal hiding places for myriads of ticks. These parasitic pests can torture the animal keenly. No hide is ever so thick and tough but that some African tick can burrow into it. But the rhino's miseries are considerably lessened by the tick bird. They are quiet looking little fellows, about the size of a catbird, but they get in much effective work. Sometimes they are known as 'the red-beaked ox-feeder'; for they also feed on the ticks infesting domestic cattle. These hungry little birds explore every fold and crease of the rhino's heavy hide, ridding him of the many ticks which molest the mighty beast.

The rhinoceros does not merely tolerate the tick birds. He cherishes them as 'permanent boarders.' The birds have an added value—they keep a keen lookout for the rhino's enemies. When a hunter appears in the offing, these sharp-eyed sentries rise instantly from the rhino's back and fly screaming about until they arouse the great drowsy beast, who will crash through the tall grass to safety, or else will charge the intruder—all according to the direction of the wind. Many a sportsman's shot has been ruined by these birds who surely pay well for their keep.

One day I happened upon a rhino as he dozed in the shade with the usual array of tick birds on his back. A second old fellow ambled leisurely into the picture. Hazily aware of an intrusion, the first animal came to attention and got under way, his charge accompanied by a whirr of wings. The newcomer, suddenly alert, rushed to meet him. Heading straight at each other, they gathered speed and force that promised a hair-raising encounter. Had the collision occurred, I should have had a priceless incident to tell. But as it happened, the story is without a climax. Within twenty feet of each other both rhinos stopped abruptly. Number one sauntered back to his tree and his tick birds, and resumed his interrupted nap. Number two proceeded on his way as if nothing had occurred.

Another time, I drew a charge from three rhinos, when I was sitting on the ground out of reach of my gun. There was nothing to do but to remain seated, and watch their approach. All three of them rushed past me at a distance of ten or fifteen feet, apparently as well satisfied with their charge as if it had resulted in my destruction.

I believe that usually the rhino's charge is merely a rush of investigation. Whenever he catches a scent, he blunders off in the direction from which it comes, just to find out what it is. The method was successful until the white man came to Africa with his rifle, because everything but an elephant or another rhino would promptly get out of the way of the great beast's onrush; and also both of these animals are large enough for even his poor eyes to see before he gets himself into trouble. However, since few men with guns have been willing to

AS THE RHINOS CHARGE WITHOUT PROVOCATION PHOTOGRAPHING
THEM IS DIFFICULT.

© A. Radclyffe Dugmore.

DUGMORE'S PHOTOGRAPHS OF CHARGING RHINOS ARE AMONG

let a rhino come within seeing distance without shooting, the result of the rhino's clumsy attacks is that these animals are being killed off in Africa.

My opinions regarding the rhino are based only on one man's experience—my own; but I have had close contact with a great number of rhinos. I have met many scores of them and have been charged many times; but as I think back over my experiences, I can recall but one case where possibly the charge was in earnest. A single shot turned the beast. Yet many men have been killed, and I have every reason to believe that the rhinos of some regions are more truculent and purposeful than those I have met and that their percentage of bluff is considerably lower.

My old friend, one of the greatest students and lovers of African wild life, Major A. Radclyffe Dugmore, has had many interesting encounters with rhinos. His photographs are certainly among the best ever made in Africa. Once, near the Nanuyuki River, he came upon a pair of rhinos and succeeded in making a short film of the old one. "But she did not behave as I wished," he said. "We saw her lying asleep under a large thorn tree and stalked her until we were within about sixty yards when a current of air carried our scent to her, whereupon she promptly got up, turned round and round, snorting and putting her tail up to show that she was alarmed; but of course she did all this on the farther side of a small thorn bush, so that I could not get a clear view of her. I moved slightly to one side with my cinema camera, expecting that she would make a dash in my direction and that I should be able to make a really good film of her and then dodge behind a big tree when she came too close for comfort. My plan was right enough, but she decided not to interview me at closer quarters. Instead she turned, and going in a comical zig-zag fashion, soon disappeared in the bush."

On another occasion Dugmore saw a group of three rhinos standing on the top of a low hill. Making a wide detour he and his companion walked toward the animals, a fine-looking bull, a cow and a youngster half-grown. Outlined against the sky, their dark gray bodies were in strong relief to the rich golden yellow grass.

"With the utmost caution," he says, "we got nearer and nearer, the camera ready for action and my companion, De Bruin, ready with his small-bore rifle. I carried no weapon more deadly than the camera, because I did not want to have any temptation to shoot, even in self defense. If the animals charged, I must take my chance, as I was determined not to kill. I had left my rifle behind. With the three great beasts in front of me, I wondered whether I had been wise. I do not mind one rhino, as it is possible to dodge if he charges; but with three, the gentle art of dodging becomes somewhat complicated. A cow with her calf is a much more serious proposition than two or more full-grown ones, and a whole family has a way of making one feel somewhat uneasy.

"When we got within a hundred yards, the wind carried a suggestion of scent to the animals. The old bull stood as still as a statue, the cow became mildly agitated and turned from side to side, her calf close beside her. The young have better eyesight than the older ones, and the comical little fellow stared at us wondering what we were. Then the youngster, thinking his fears were groundless, lay down while his parents kept a careful watch. Unfortunately, though approaching from the safest direction, I was not in proper range. So down on all fours we went, moving twenty yards to one side and farther forward. Now I made some more pictures with the three animals posed in a compact group. A current of air next carried our scent the wrong way, and the old cow and her calf became greatly alarmed. In a comical way they swung round and round, with tails held straight up as danger signals. Fortunately the breeze changed again. The baby suddenly remembered that he had had nothing to eat for a long time, and so he rushed to his mother and took his dinner."

At last, needing action for the camera, Dugmore suggested to De Bruin that he fire a shot into the ground near the animals. The ringing shot made the great beasts jump about. They headed straight for the camera. Dugmore continued to turn the crank, obtaining a splendid film. The naturalist finishes the story by saying, "What was to happen to the camera I scarcely dared think. I was too busy wondering what would happen to me. But all my fears and worries soon vanished, for the three frantic creatures suddenly turned for some unknown reason and I got a splendid view of them disappearing with marvellous speed over the top of the hill. Never have I enjoyed anything so much as photographing their tail view." [1]

But Africa is not the only home of the rhino. They are found in India and in the Indo-Malayan regions. The Indian animal is the largest of the Asiatic rhinos. The first live rhino ever sent to Europe, since the days of the Roman shows, was sent from India to Emmanuel, King of Portugal, in 1573. And it was from a sketch taken in Lisbon that Albert Dürer composed his celebrated but fanciful engraving, which has been reproduced in so many old books on natural history. This Indian rhino has been hunted by breaking him out of the jungle with a line of elephants. The Javan rhino is much smaller than the Indian beast and has an extensive range, being found near Calcutta, Burma, the Malay Peninsula, Java, Sumatra and Borneo, where it chooses to inhabit the wooded hilly countries rather than the grassy jungles.

There are two kinds of rhino in Africa: the black

[1] A. R. Dugmore: "The Wonderland of Big Game."

rhino, which I have been telling about, and his extremely rare brother, the white rhino. It is sometimes called Burchell's Rhinoceros. Unlike the black rhino, who has a prehensile upper lip-feeler for feeding on bushes and long tufts of grass, the white rhino has a square mouth adapted to cropping grass. It is therefore found in open countries and where there are broad grassy meadows between the strips of bush. Years ago, the white rhino was frequently seen in South Africa, but now they are quite extinct south of the Zambesi, except in Zululand, where, according to latest reports, there are twelve which are strictly preserved. Today, a few white rhinos exist in the British Protectorate of Uganda north of Victoria Nyanza and also a very few in the Belgian Congo. In both regions the rare beast is protected.

Because they are somewhat larger than the black rhino, sportsmen have always been eager to shoot them. Occasionally other men report having seen a white rhino in regions far away from their usual habitat, but invariably they prove to be black rhinos covered with the dust of the white mud in which they have been wallowing. I saw one such near the Northern Eusso Nyiro. At a distance, and with the sun shining on him, he looked a pale grayish-white.

When either running or walking, the white rhino holds its head very low, its nose almost touching the ground. Like elephants, they feed during the night and in the cool hours of early morning and evening. The great hunter, the late Frederick Courtenay Selous, has related that when a small white rhino calf accompanies its mother it always runs in front and she appears to guide it by holding the point of her horn upon the little animal's rump; and that when the mother changes her pace from a trot to a gallop, the same position is always maintained.

The double horns of a rhino are not attached closely to the skull, as in the case of most horned animals. They are really protuberances on his hide. A record black rhino horn measures 53½ inches, and a white, 62½ (female), while an average horn will not measure more than 20 in the black and 30 in the white. The horns bring a high price and are frequently sent to China, where they are said to be used for medicinal purposes.

Rhinos begin their blundering career quite early in life. Late one afternoon, at the end of a march down the Tana River from Fort Hall, I sat in front of my camp in my steamer chair, dozing and dreaming that I was listening to the violent squealing of pigs. As the racket grew louder and louder, I sat up wide awake, and realized that the squealing was a reality. The noise was just below camp and grew steadily nearer. Before I had time to investigate, several porters came into view carrying a long pole. Trussed to the middle of the pole was a black mass, kicking as hard as it was squealing. It was a baby rhino—and he was certainly an ugly little fellow. One of my companions, wandering a little way from camp into the thorn bush, had discovered the young rhino. The boys had captured it, and the commotion had begun at once. The mother, feeding only a little way off, now came snorting and charging in to protect her offspring. A rifle shot had hurt her only slightly, but it was enough to make her turn and plunge off into the jungle. The pole was then cut, the abandoned baby slung on it, and the noisy procession set out for camp.

For the next few days, the unruly infant kept us all busy. An improvised nursing bottle was rigged up and filled with milk, and we all took turns offering it to him in an attempt to make friends. But for a long time we did not approach beyond the limits of his tether, for the little wretch charged madly at anyone who came near him. And if there was no one near by whom he could charge, he threw himself at the tree to which he was tied—snorting and squealing, true to the traditional instincts of the rhino. After a time, however, he became friendly, and, eventually, entirely docile. In spite of their blustering dispositions, baby rhinos may become gentle and even somewhat affectionate pets.

Another baby rhino gave me an unforgettable surprise one morning as I was crossing a flat covered with dense grass as high as my head. I was leading the *safari*, spreading the grass apart with my hands to make a path for my boys to follow. I soon reached a little gully three or four feet deep and just about as wide. It was quite hidden until I was right upon it. I soon found a convenient boulder in the middle of the gully and started to use it as a stepping stone. Pushing the grass aside to get a better view of my landing place, I reached my foot toward the boulder just as it began to move! I backed quickly, wondering if I was 'seeing things.' Then I peeped through the grass screen again and I saw that my boulder was a baby rhino. I had not frightened it; for while I waited, it moved slowly down the little gully. Fifty yards below, where the ditch ended, the baby's mother soon appeared. She did a lot of snorting and pawing about, sending my black boys scrambling up the trees. But in a moment she pushed her baby in front of her and they both galloped away.

Since the rhino will charge without provocation, it is very difficult to get close enough to him to make photographs. Because photographic records are one of the important purposes of scientific expeditions, I once undertook, before going to Africa, to construct a rhino decoy. With steel tubing, wire and a covering of burlap, I built a realistic, but inoffensive, rhino. It required two men, one inside the hind legs, the other inside the front legs, to maneuver the dummy. The one in the front who was able to look out through the snout had room to manipulate a camera placed in the head of my fake rhino. The chief difficulty was to imitate the rhino's walk. To have the legs of the dummy rhino move with the stride of a man, would have been a 'dead give-away.' Finally, I so arranged springs in the jointed legs that I secured a fair imitation of the rhino's gait. A coat of slate-colored paint, applied in camp after I reached Africa, completed the job. I was then ready to go out in rhino disguise to hunt with my camera along the banks of the Tana. It proved a knotty problem, however, to find a native willing to play the rôle of the rhino's hind legs. Therefore, I never had the chance to give my decoy a fair trial.

When I returned to America from that expedition, I left my rhino effigy stored in Nairobi with a firm of *safari* outfitters. I had quite forgotten about him until one day when Martin Johnson, about to return to Africa for his five-year photographic expedition, was in my studio talking about various sorts of blinds. He happened to mention an idea suggested to him by 'Willie.' "Who is he?" I asked. I soon discovered that Johnson referred to my old rhino decoy, which had been unearthed one day quite by accident in the Nairobi warehouse. No one had remembered to whom the thing belonged. But it was loaned to Johnson, who began to experiment with it near the town. The chief experience that the photographer got out of his day with the dummy was a good deal of amusement.

Adventures in the African Jungle

Rhinos have disappeared from the region about Nairobi. Should Johnson, keenly interested in the development of the decoy idea, take my device along to the country where real rhinos abound, perhaps we may hear an interesting story. It is even possible that some grouchy old rhino may regard the decoy as an intruding stranger and may press home a real charge.

Sometimes in African hunting a real prize is bagged quite by accident. This time, the trophy fell to another. I was camped near Lake Elementeita. Another *safari*, that of Mr. Abel Chapman and his brother, was located about a hundred yards from me on the shore of the lake. Chapman was eager to secure a hippopotamus. He hoped to kill the animal at night as it fed on shore, because salvaging a dead hippo in water is a task of enormous difficulty. The moon was long past its full. The hunters retired early, leaving instructions to be called when it should rise.

Shortly after midnight they were awakened by an *askari* who told them that a hippo was close to camp. The whinnying of a pony had given the alarm. Drawing on coats and field shoes, and summoning their gun boys, Chapman and his brother hurried out of their tents. The night was still gray and starry, but they could easily make out the shadowy form of a great beast about three hundred yards distant.

Adventures in the African Jungle

When within fifty yards of the animal, Chapman dropped on one knee to take aim. With a loud snort the massive creature rushed at them. Both men fired. One gun boy, knowing that the snort and charge did not belong to a hippo, fled into camp. The other gun boy stood firm. Fortunately a second gun was unnecessary. On came the beast another five yards. Then he dropped, plowing up the ground with his snout as he fell.

From the camp the boys now hurried out with lights so that the hunters might inspect their hippo. Then it was that Chapman discovered they had killed not a hippo at all, but an unusually fine rhino bearing three horns. It was a beautiful specimen and a very rare one indeed. For days I had been looking in this country for just such a rhino and, ironically enough, the prize of the whole region had deliberately walked into the camp of my neighbors.

The shot that brought down the big tri-horn was one of the best. Crashing into the neck between the ears, and smashing into the spinal column, it narrowly missed the great horns as the rhino charged forward headlong. No bullet aimed in broad daylight ever did its work more effectively. Had the shot been less fortunate, the wounded and infuriated rhino might easily have done so much damage that he would have impaired seriously my belief in the bluff of the rhino. The prize was lost to me, but my theory remained safe. Gladly, however, would I have traded all my pet theories for that rhino— one of the most desirable specimens ever obtained by any hunter in all Africa.

CHAPTER XI   BOB

BY MARY L. JOBE AKELEY

BOB was a little, chubby-faced Baganda boy the color of ebony. He might have been ten or eleven years old when I first saw him, but his age always puzzled me. As I came to know him better, he often seemed not much more than eight or nine, so innocent was he and almost baby-like. Again, when he tackled a man's job and felt hurt when ordered to let a stronger boy do it, or when he would undergo the physical hardships of the trail without even a murmur, then he appeared much older. But there was no way to tell. Birthdays do not count in Bob's tribe, and there is no way to date them if they did. Bob was born and had lived all his life in a land where time stands still, where the only seasons you can notice are the periods of long rains and short rains and the dry weeks in between. Bob dwelt on the Equator where there is no spring, summer, autumn nor winter, and where no

[235]

account is kept of the months; where there is no Easter, no Thanksgiving, nor even Christmas.

And yet in the year 1926, Bob brought me the only Christmas present I received. I was tramping with a *safari* of three hundred natives out of the Belgian Congo. My heart was stricken with grief and loneliness, for after working side by side with my husband for eight months on this *my first trip to Africa,* I had seen him start on that long journey from which no wanderer returns. For six weeks I had camped beside his new-made grave in the gorilla land he loved, in order to complete his unfinished tasks. Now I had come down from the volcanoes, and on this Christmas day I had covered eighteen of the hundred long and weary miles between our high camp on the slopes of Mt. Mikeno and the end of the road at Kabale where we had stored our motors on the way into the Congo.

For eight hours I had trudged with our faithful gun boy, Bill, and the old Swahili porter, Thomasi, along the tree-shaded highway, bordered by *shambas* of ripe bananas and fields of peas bright with their variegated blossoms—for the common edible peas of Africa bloom in as many lovely colors as our own sweet peas—and at last I had reached our old camp ground at Kisola in the late afternoon. The chief and his retinue were there to meet me, offering me many expressions of kindness and of

[236]

Adventures in the African Jungle

sympathy and urging me to tell them how they could be of service to me.

"We go now, *Memsahib*," said the chiefs. "We wish you to rest well and sleep the night through. We come back when the sun comes again. We wish to help you." Then occurred the event of the day. A handsome little black boy came up to my chair where I was finishing my tea. His beautifully modeled body was naked save for a little black and white spotted goat skin swinging from one shoulder. He looked straight at me and smiled— smiled with his big, shining black eyes and with his childish mouth, showing his white and perfect teeth. With his chubby hands he offered me a basket of luscious ripe red strawberries which he had been carrying porter-fashion on his head.

"For *Memsahib*," he said in his native Kenyaruanda dialect, "and I hope she has good health." Then he stood at attention, smiling, his heels snapped together like a little soldier, his chest held high and his back straight as an arrow. I have never seen a child of more beautiful physique. His head was well shaped and he carried it like a little prince.

The child then ran away, but very soon came back, offering me another hand woven basket of brilliant colors. This one contained freshly shelled green peas. A troop of small boys of all shades of black and brown followed him, one or two with baskets of newly picked, tender green beans, which they placed on the ground in front of me. It was thus in the guise of Santa Claus that Bob introduced himself to me.

But there was something far more important than my presents, I soon noticed. All these native children, including Bob, were dancing about, chattering and laughing in great excitement. Finally Bob came up to me.

"*Memsahib*, I wish to go on *safari* with you," he said, "I wish to go on as far as you go." The news of the thousand mile journey I still had to undertake had evidently reached the ears of these youngsters. They probably had never heard of Central Uganda, nor the Great Rift Valley, nor Nairobi, the metropolis of East Africa, whither I was ultimately bound, but they knew I had to make a long *safari*. "I wish to stay as long as you stay. I want to go with you to see a new country," little Bob pleaded and stood his ground watching me carefully.

What a Christmas gift indeed! But it was far too good to be true, I thought. Early in our African journey, my husband had asked me if I would like to have a cunning little water spaniel I had admired in Nairobi. If so, he had said I could have a little *toto* to look after it, and both would be company for me if I were ever left alone in camp. But, as events proved, I was never alone in camp, being always with my husband in his collecting in

[238]

the field, so both the dog and the *toto* had been forgotten.

Now this appealing little fellow was offering to come into my service. He touched me deeply. Certainly it would not be allowed to take such a young child from his district. The chief, or the boy's parents, or the District Commissioner would surely object. However, in his eagerness, the child's quick mind had covered all these points. He immediately brought up to me the chief's headman, and, sure enough, the headman told me that the little boy could go with me if I wished him to do so.

"But what will your father and mother say?" Bill asked him.

The little boy darted out beyond the palisade of young trees enclosing the rest-house grounds and reappeared leading a very old woman by the hand. He said, "This is my grandmother. She will speak for my family. My father is away on business for the chief, and my mother must stay in her *shamba* with her young baby. The baby is too small for my mother to bring with her or to leave behind."

The old grandmother was clothed only in conventional goat skin but she was adorned with many large hoop-shaped earrings and she wore heavy armlets, leglets and necklaces of copper wire. She seated herself without invitation in one of our little folding canvas chairs and soon was puffing away at one of Bill's cigarettes. She sat thus for a long time without speaking but she watched me intently. The boy stood patiently waiting. Finally she told me she would be very pleased if I would take with me her little grandson, the little Mihigo, as he was called.

But in my mind the most important question was still unsettled. How would the child be returned to his tribe? At this point, my Baganda cook stepped forward. The palaver had interested all our personal boys and had extended even to Enoka's kitchen. "As soon as your *safari* is finished, *Memsahib*," he said, "I will come back to Kabale to my father's home. With me I will bring the little boy to the District Commissioner, who if you request him will surely send the child back to the chief at Kisola."

Thus it was fated that little Mihigo, 'the Hunter,' whose hut and *shamba* were perched high on 'Chintale,' the 'Hill of the Lion,' among the blue mountains of Western Uganda, should go with me as my personal *toto* to the end of our *safari*. I called him 'Bob' immediately—it was so much easier to say and to remember—precisely as Carl had named Uimbia Gikingu 'Bill' when he, just such a little boy as this, Bill told me, had begged to join 'the *Bwana's safari*,' twenty years before.

Bright and early the next morning while we were gathering around our table to eat our breakfasts by lantern light, Bob marched into camp. He carried a short

[240]

bamboo cane tipped with a metal point and he had a tiny bundle tied up in bright red cotton cloth, about the size of a quart measure, perched on top of his head. He had brought with him all his worldly possessions—a little drinking calabash (gourd) and a few pennies in British currency—for barring the goat skin, Bob's wardrobe was only the enveloping sunshine and the cooling breeze.

The child squatted down on the ground near by and never once took his eyes off me. He was respectful in the extreme but he watched every move I made. He had for all the world the vigilant attitude of a faithful dog who fears his master may forget and leave him behind. Perhaps he thought I might change my mind and tell him he could not go.

We were on the march before dawn. All the long morning, we climbed up and up over the steep hills flanking the lower country, and Bob was never more than half a dozen paces behind me. Bill, who carried the big elephant gun, or even Thomasi who carried my water bottle and few personal things, might walk next to me, but I was sure that Bob was right on their heels. He was swift on his feet and quick as a cat in his every movement.

From the beginning, Bob began to anticipate my needs and would surprise me by dragging my water bottle off old Thomasi's shoulder and bringing it up to me at every halt we made in the long hard climb. I soon recognized that if I had adopted Bob into my *safari* he had surely adopted me into his young heart.

But the greatest fun of this day and of every other day while we were on porter *safari,* was at the end of the march when I had to pay off the porters. It was eleven o'clock—six hours after our start—that we reached camp in a table-like clearing on the high mountain at Behungi. We were glad to get into the shade of the rest-house porch, for the sun, now almost on the meridian, was blazing out of a cloudless sky.

Our three hundred porters, their powerful bodies shining with oil and dripping with perspiration, had dropped their loads in a low banda under the direction of Bill and our head man, Makasudi. Then they had flocked out, forming in a crowded line eager for their forty cents in Uganda currency (ten cents in United States money) the tariff for carrying fifty pounds fifteen miles. I had several canvas bags of small coins, and it was my habit to pour them out in an old wash basin from which I could count and pay more quickly.

Bob now began to show his helpfulness. He marshalled the porters into line, reproved them for crowding. "Get in line there you big *mpagazi* (porter). One at a time. No push, no crowd. *Kwenda* (go, get out)! You get your *mshahara* (wages). You get pay plenty. *Kwenda,* you big *mpagazi!*" Then *"Santa"* (thank you), he would shout in his childish treble, and as soon as they were paid, *"Kwenda,"* rapping on the ground with his little bamboo cane. He both got and gave many a laugh, for the porters were all from Kisola, his own country. He waved the last *"Qua-heri"* (farewell) as they dog-trotted down the hill on the return trip to their *shambas,* apparently not the least fatigued by their morning's labor.

That day, as we had climbed up through the bamboos near the camp ground, we had come upon a sad and terrified native limping along in the opposite direction. He was weeping and moaning at every step. His face was dripping with blood. Bill questioned him: "What *piga* (hurt you)?" He replied. *"Tembo piga. Tembo piga mpagazi. Tembo kutinda* (kill)." An elephant had attacked him and had killed his companion in the forest, a few hundred yards below, where they had been cutting bamboo.

The next morning we saw where the tragedy had occurred. The bamboos were uprooted, twisted about and trampled into the soft earth. The ground was torn up as if by shell fire, while strewn along the trail for many yards were gruesome fragments of the poor native's body. We all went through on the double quick. The gun boys were on the alert. Bill, with the elephant gun ready for action, kept between me and the danger zone. Bob was close on my heels, sprinting through at a round pace, and having all his eyes about him. It was a big thrill for Bob, as well as for the rest of us. However, in fairness to the 'bad elephant,' I must say here that he had turned 'rogue' only after he had been persecuted for several weeks by the natives with their poisoned arrows.

That day's trek had been almost interminable. Our trail had led up and down heavily forested mountains, across sun-baked swamp lands and along recent hippo trails, where a large herd of these prehistoric survivals had plowed through the soft or flooded lowlands. We had labored through another fifteen miles when, in the early afternoon, we reached lovely Lake Bunyoni. All the natives in their little grass huts along the lake were agog, for His Excellency, the Governor of Uganda, had been spending Christmas there. After a hasty lunch we packed our dunnage into a fleet of dugouts and the stalwart boatmen transported us among islands of enchantment across Bunyoni's waters—green and blue and filled with masses of purple lotus with shining golden hearts. It was Bob's first boat ride. It was also his first glimpse of fish leaping in the sunlight before our speeding canoes.

The next morning was full of excitement. We were only seven miles from where our motors were waiting for us. Long before daylight our Kabale porters had thrown up their head loads. Swinging back and forth along the line, half a dozen lanterns lighted the way in that heavy darkness which just precedes the dawn. We were on the last stretch of our march from the Congo.

It was downgrade nearly all the way, and for part of the way I decided to try the chair which, up to that time, I had not used in Africa. I had preferred to be physically tired and somehow I had felt a reluctance to being carried. But these sturdy Uganda porters now ran along chattering and singing as if they carried no load at all. They were nearly all six feet tall, strong and keen, and as zestful as if they were on a holiday. And Bob, flourishing his small bamboo cane in the rhythm of the bearers' stride, happy and important as any drum-major, pattered along beside us on a smooth and narrow footpath as I was swept onward in my chair. *"Kwenda, kwenda,"* he would shout in glee. *"Kwenda, Upesi! Upesi sana!"* (Come quick! Very quick!) It was a gala day for Bob. Then he would sing to himself "Tum-te-tum-te-tum" in perfect time with the porters' lively feet. Today joyous music was singing in his ears and dancing in his childish heart.

The gorilla guide, Mguru, had wished to accompany me from the Congo to Kabale, and I had secured permission from his government for the journey and had arranged for his safe return. Bill was glad to have him, as they had become great friends, and Mguru was always helpful in getting the *safari* on the road early in

[245]

Adventures in the African Jungle

the morning. This guide was greatly attached to me and constantly sought me out to render me some kindly little service. The last two or three days before we reached Kabale, Mguru had told me frequently that he wanted to ride in my motor car. Although he was probably thirty years old, he had never seen a settlement larger than the government posts of Rutshuru and Kisenyi. Now the two short streets of Kabale, lined with *dukas*, with their Indian venders and their display of bright cottons and gleaming tin ware, and the motor roads over which lorries and *safari* cars pass occasionally, amazed this simple Kivu guide. But if these sights and sounds fascinated Mguru, they completely bewildered little Bob, who had never seen even Rutshuru. In fact he had never seen a shop, a bolt of 'Americani,' a tin of petrol, or even an ox-cart.

Bob's eyes were a glowing wonder. If his little woolly head had not been so closely cropped, I think his hair would have been constantly on end. His little brain was in such a whirl at these novel experiences that he could not say a word for the first half day. He just gazed at the new world in which he suddenly found himself.

Bob was more than excited while my car was being put in commission. Not an hour in the day passed but he would refer to it by some little word or sign. Finally the car was ready. Perched on Mguru's knee beside

Adventures in the African Jungle

me in the front seat, that they might not miss anything, Bob took his first motor ride. Their squeals of nervous delight as the engine turned over and the car glided along the road I shall never forget. "Ai! Ai! Ai!" they cried excitedly, "Motor car! Motor car!" It was all a mystery, a mystery too profound for them even to attempt to understand. The mirrors, the lights, the horn—all held them spellbound. If I had allowed Mguru and Bob free rein, the satisfaction of their curiosity might have done serious damage to my car.

When our motor *safari* was finally ready to roll down the long hill from the District Commissioner's headquarters at Kabale, Bob was envied by more than one of the native boys who watched our departure, certainly by poor Mguru waving his crownless straw hat in reluctant farewell while his face was wet with tears. I had taken the wheel of my husband's heavily laden motor lorry, and Bob sat on the front seat between Bill and me. He was an eager, triumphant little soul. His constant joy and wonderment were proving a real diversion to me.

But Bob was by no means content to be merely a good humored hanger on. He had taken on a job, and early in the game it became evident that he intended to perform his duties to the best of his ability. It had been agreed that his pay was to be five shillings a month. Of course, his food was to be furnished him, just as in the case of the other boys and porters. The first night he told me he needed a 'blanketty' the full right of every boy in the white man's service. But, he assured me, he would need only one thin one—the other boys require two—as he intended to sleep close to Bill. I gave him the blanket. At Kabale some natives had brought in grass mats for sale. He had asked for one costing two shillings. "Please *Memsahib*, give me mat. Ground *baridi, baridi sana* (cold—very cold)," he begged. Needless to say he got the mat as well. So Bob's possessions were being gradually —if sparingly—increased. His little bundle was always loaded and off-loaded with Bill's, and he tagged along with Bill as if the gun boy had been his father.

Bob early began to assume some of my personal boy's duties. Shortly after my tent had been erected at Kabale, and I was resting a little before changing to clean cloth-ing, the child appeared with a large basin full of hot water and proceeded to remove my heavy boots and stockings. Then, squatting on the ground tailor fashion, he began to bathe my feet. I was surprised to find how clever he was. He rubbed my feet, manipulating each toe in turn with the skill of a masseur. When he had fin-ished, and had gently dried my feet, he sat looking at me for the approval I quickly gave.

"And where did you learn how to care for tired feet?" I asked.

"Oh, I was once a *toto* for an Englishman," Bob proudly replied.

Adventures in the African Jungle

I blessed the Englishman, not once but many times thereafter, for Bob, finding how acceptable the service was, took upon himself this office of devotion.

But it was at Kampala that Bob's duties increased. There I paid off several of our East African personal boys, whom I sent by boat and rail to Nairobi. This was necessary not only because our loads required lightening but chiefly because these boys, trained by a score and more of white masters, were tired of the long *safari* and had become stale on their jobs. Thereafter, with the exception of Bill, I had only native speaking boys, who were quite unspoiled and consequently formed the best *safari* we had on the whole expedition.

Bob now helped constantly in the care of my tent. He helped to roll up my bed and pack my dunnage in the morning and to make my bed and unpack in the evening. He kept my wash basin filled with clean water. He helped to serve our meals and to wash and dry the dishes. He was a proud little fellow as he darted about setting the table, carrying a hot dish or flourishing the red-striped dish towel in the air.

If Kampala proved the beginning of a new epoch in Bob's duties, it also marked a new chapter in Bob's personal experiences and desires. Kampala is the chief city of Uganda. In it dwell whites, Indians and natives. There are many sightly homes with beautifully kept and spacious English gardens. There is a broad and long thoroughfare, lined with English shops, affording all the necessities and many of the luxuries of Colonial life. There is also a large native market, where fruits and vegetables and cereals, eggs and meat and poultry and live sheep are sold.

To all of these new sights Bob registered persistent amazement. But it was the crowded Indian bazaar, filled with brilliant color, fragrant spicy odors and noxious smells, that held him enthralled. He stared at the Indians with their curious costumes and the shops filled with strange wares from an alien land. He looked askance at black and buxom native belles garbed in brilliant draperies of gaily patterned calicoes and bearing on their heads large baskets of steaming rice—a marked contrast to his sisters at home whose only garment was a goat skin softened with oil and earth, and who carried their burdens in skin bags hung low on their backs.

But the special objects of his wondering gaze were the half-grown black children, sucking joints of sugar cane and gazing longingly at little open dukas containing piles of greasy sweet meats and unfamiliar porridges and thick brown soup in heavy black pots, the counterparts of our own 'hot dog' stands. Bob's gaze was one of astonishment and of envy as well, as I very soon realized, for these little black boys were not clad in goat skin as he was. They were all wearing little cotton shirts and shorts. I felt Bob crouching down a little as he sat be-

Adventures in the African Jungle

side me in the shelter of my motor car. We had to stay in Kampala three days, as we were shipping out some of our collection by boat and rail freight. Those three days were almost the mental undoing of Bob. He soon began to whisper to Bill. Then came his direct request to me. *"Memsahib,* I want clothes—clothes like these other little boys wear." I pretended not to understand. Then, as he insisted, I told him I liked him much better as he was.

"But," he remonstrated, with perfectly good reasoning, "no other little boy in this country wears a goat skin. They all wear clothes." There was no denying it. If he could possibly manage it, Bob intended to behave in Rome as the Romans do. I finally had to tell him that my chief reason for taking him on my *safari* was because he did not dress like a white boy, nor an Indian boy, nor one of these little native boys that try to look like white boys; that I took him because he was a proper Baganda boy. But it was not until after we had said good-by to Kampala with its gay thoroughfares and its temptations and had reached the outlying country where the native children wear almost no clothing at all, just as God meant all his black children who dwell on the Equator to do, that Bob lost his self-consciousness and became his normal happy self again.

Three days after we left Kampala we were caught in a heavy downpour of rain. We had wanted to go far

[251]

that day, but, unable to reach a proper camp ground, we had stopped beside the broad highway and there had hung up lanterns for head and tail lights on our motors and, like a band of gypsies, had pitched our tents in the easiest and quickest way.

It had been a long hard day for all of us. I told the boys to pitch for me my little Whymper tent just large enough for my cot and chair. I turned in as soon as possible after a light supper. I was just dozing off when I became aware of something crawling into my tent. A squeaky, almost tearful, little voice said *"Memsahib,"* and Bob rolled himself up in his blanket across the doorway. The night was cold and damp. I remembered that the red felt sun-canopy for my tent had been unpacked with my blankets. I found it in the dark, without getting up, and threw it over Bob who had gone to sleep the moment he had lain down. From that night on, during the next six weeks in the field, Bob slept across the door of my tent, though he never explained his reason, and he invariably rolled himself up in my red sun-canopy. Sometimes on a cold night I would hear him edging under the foot of my bed for protection, and as before I would throw him some additional covering. The nights were much less lonely with this little black boy as my self-appointed protector, who himself still needed a mother's care.

Finally we came to the last lap of our African expedition. We had reached the Great Rift Valley. It was desperately hot—the only uncomfortable heat I experienced in more than a year in Africa. Our thermometer would have registered 120° F. in the shade had there been any shade, but at the Evans' seisal farm, where we left our heavily laden motors, there was only a treeless meadow for a camping ground. We were used to camping in open places. In fact we always selected such a spot by choice, because it is usually only in damp and shaded places that ticks and other disease-bearing insects lurk. But here the heat was almost unbearable, because we had so recently come from our eleven thousand foot camp in the Kivu, where in the mornings we had walked out on the hoar frost and had broken ice in our water jars. It was *ninety degrees hotter here* in the Great Rift at sunrise than it had been in the gorilla mountains.

Miles of rocky, arid country, we had no idea how many, lay between us and our goal, Lake Hannington, near which Carl had planned to secure plant accessories and to have our artist paint the background for a group of greater koodoo for the American Museum of Natural History. The great valley is inhabited only by a few native Kamasia herders, and it is passable only on foot or by donkey train. There were now no donkeys available as there had been when my husband had first journeyed here. In fact I had the greatest difficulty in securing even a handful of Kamasia porters for the trip. As for getting a local guide who knew the country, it was out of the question. The best we could do was to follow the general advice of natives who worked on the seisal farm, and the Kamasia porters we had secured, not one of whom had a first-hand knowledge of the route. The journey into this hostile region of almost unbearable heat, of difficult travel over jagged rocks, would have been unendurable but for the purpose that ever drove us onward. The work my husband had left unfinished remained ours to do. Loyalty to him and to his serious undertaking gave us courage for our task.

Our particular objective was that part of the basin of Lake Hannington where the Eastern Escarpment rises abruptly to the high table land. There, in the days before the deadly disease, rinderpest, broke out, many greater koodoo had roamed at will. The lake itself, my husband had told me, was an exquisite turquoise blue and thousands of flamingoes dotted its placid surface like shifting rose-colored islands.

Although I had telegraphed ahead to the District Commissioner at Eldama Ravine, to engage an adequate number of porters for me, it had been of no avail. Porters in that part of Africa are today almost unknown. All errands are done by motor transport, and no white man for many years had desired to undergo the hardships of tramping into Lake Hannington. I was everywhere discouraged in my proposed attempt to finish this

Photo. by R. H. Rockwell.

MARY L. JOBE AKELEY IN HER WORK TENT IN AFRICA.

BOB.

part of our expedition's job. However, on our arrival at Eldama, I found by merest chance that a few native Kamasia had just finished cutting grass at the government post. After much persuasion on the part of the District Commissioner and myself, I finally recruited seventeen, all told. They had marched across country and had awaited us at the Evans' ranch. With so few porters, we had to travel in relays, taking in all the necessities for half our force on the first trip and returning for the remainder of the party with a minimum of equipment. We cut down our outfit and supplies to the last ounce, and took up the trail. Even at sunrise the earth was blasted with heat. We continued in a general direction toward Lake Hannington, though the most intelligent of the Kamasia soon declared he had not much idea as to how to reach the lake.

Fifteen years had elapsed since Bill, upon whose experience we had come to rely, had visited the lake. His memory of the valley was vague. My husband had given me a somewhat detailed account of the region in which he expected to work, so I knew the main object was to get to the lake.

As we traveled steadily downgrade into a lower altitude, it became hotter. Through my heavy tramping boots the sun's penetrating rays and the burning, sharp, volcanic slag soon blistered and cooked my feet. Occasionally a greet spot in the distance invited us to hurry on, with promise of rest in the shade, but when we reached it we found the trees almost bare, with the sun striking fiercely through the nearly leafless branches. Bill, with the frugality born of experience, doled out the rain water with which Mrs. Evans, our hostess at the seisal farm, had generously filled our bottles from her own nearly exhausted supply.

All our East African boys, who had been with us for almost a year in the field, were nearly overcome. They dragged themselves along groaning and complaining of the heat and the jagged rocks at almost every step. The recently recruited Kamasia found their loads almost more than they could manage. They are slim and lightly built, and not at all as sturdy as either Swahili or Baganda porters.

By nightfall we had traveled fifteen miles, but not once had we seen Lake Hannington. We pitched our camp where the steaming waters of a dozen hot springs pour into the Lower Molo. There was no need for Bob to heat water for my bath that night. Mother Earth kept her hot water faucets running at full capacity. The child staggered in with a basin full of steaming water. I waited a long time for it to cool sufficiently for bathing my now badly swollen feet. Bob literally fell down in his tracks a few yards away, to get the sleep his tired little body needed.

We had a night of true tropic heat. I had only my

mosquito canopy and one thin sheet over me, and slept with the moon beating full upon me. I think I should have suffocated had I tried to sleep in my tent. We awoke unrefreshed, to take up a trail leading steadily downward and again into regions of still greater heat.

After only two hours of travel our porters halted at a little river. The water was only slightly brackish and it flowed in the deep shade of wild fig trees. They were unanimous in their wish not to go further in the heat. "We do not wish to get to the 'salt water,' " as they called the lake. They splashed about in the river. It required a big effort for Bill and me to drive the heat-tortured *safari* to the sun-baked trail again.

We had traveled perhaps four miles when we sighted Lake Hannington, not at the southern end as I had hoped, but at the extreme northern end of the lake. The lake was filled with flamingoes, and the prospect was beautiful indeed, but the discouraging fact remained that we were now undeniably as far from where I wished to pitch our permanent camp as we had been when we had started the day before. Instead of taking a direct route to the lake, our uncertain guide had chosen the well defined caravan route to Lake Baringo which touches Lake Hannington at this point. At any rate, I thought, I had found the flamingoes at their best and I should get some fine photographs. I looked around everywhere for my camera boys. They were nowhere in sight. One or two porters who finally caught up with us reported that the camera boys had started on the trail and then, unknown to any of us, had returned to the river, five miles away to wait there until the heat should abate. They had become wholly demoralized.

Just as the sun dropped behind a pile of black clouds, the only clouds we saw at Lake Hannington, and for that day at least making photography impossible, the slackers arrived. My opportunity had gone. To photograph the flamingoes I would either have to spend another day here or else make a return trip. As I could not wait the extra day without seriously impeding the work of the expedition, we started on down the lake, fatigued and footsore though we were and quite tired enough to camp.

We traveled in and out along the broken shore. Five miles farther on, near a clear but alkaline spring, we made camp. The water was a godsend because we had only a 'debbie' of water left—far too little to see us through the evening and the following day.

As night approached, the landscape became alive with birds. Great numbers of flamingoes flew low over the water in long pink streaks against the blue-green background of the lake. Above them big black-winged pelicans flew in massed formations. All during the sunset and twilight hours they traveled swiftly by, calling incessantly in a babel of racket. The flamingoes feed in the

Adventures in the African Jungle

shallows, scooping up the minute life from the mud flats with their long trough-like bills in a peculiar side-sweeping motion, like a regiment of pink-clad chamber-maids on stilts vigorously mopping up some vast muddied floor. The plumage of these lovely creatures is chiefly a pale rose color, but flame-colored feathers on wings and breast make the bird seem a vivid pink.

That night a light rain fell, accompanied by sharp squalls which nearly blew our tents down. The hippos had come in near our tiny spring, to feed on the little green forage remaining there. Now they were sloshing about at the water's edge, alternately rising to the sur-face and then snorting and diving out of sight again.

Next morning as we traveled on down the rocky shore of the lake, it seemed hotter than the day before. The sun glared and reflected from the still waters. All along, the shore line was encrusted with a deposit of salts, mingled with feathers and bones of flamingoes. The stench from the thick, foul waters was nauseating. We now understood why the white settlers of the Lower Molo had not wished to visit the lake, and why they had discouraged me in my undertaking.

At last we reached the boiling springs five miles from the southern end of the lake. The sun was so intense that I could not look into the steaming waters. Fortu-nately these springs were a landmark for Bill, who immediately recognized an old trail that Carl had used fifteen years before. I now waited with the *safari,* finding a little shade under the overhanging trunk of a giant fig tree. I stretched up a small sheet of canvas as an extra shade, and here Bob and I threw ourselves down and waited while Bill went off to investigate. Bob was very quiet. His little face was gaunt and drawn, and Bill had told me that the child had eaten little since we had started into the valley. The porters found a little water hole and splashed about in it but Bob lay prone on the ground beside me.

Bill, now followed the familiar path which led up to a cattle *manyatta.* Here he hoped to recruit a native guide, since it was imperative that we waste no more time or strength in finding my husband's old camp ground, where there was a supply of decent water. When Bill approached the huts, all the men ran away and hid. Only a woman and a few children greeted him. But Bill was used to the tricks of the native and scouted around until he found one sturdy middle-aged man hiding under a bed.

"Kinge hapa, baba," (come here, father.) Bill had urged; and when Bill finally routed him out he whined repeatedly, *"Mimi mzee, Mimi mzee,"* (I am an old man, I am an old man). He mistook Bill for an agent of the District Commissioner. As the young and able-bodied Kamasia herders are often drafted for government work,

it is a favorite ruse to escape such labor by declaring themselves old and decrepit.

But the 'old man' did not throw any dust in Bill's eyes. Bill stuck to his point. He told the native we needed him to guide us to water and finally the old fellow consented.

It was high noon when Bill and the Kamasia returned to us. We started on immediately, crossing a wide plain of brick colored volcanic ash, following along the bed of a sandy *donga* with thorn bushes growing thick above our heads and shutting out every bit of air. Beyond this we came to high, dry grass, through which we had to beat our way; then on up toward boulder-piled hills.

For only five minutes at a time would Bill permit us to rest under some tree whose thin foliage cast a scanty shade. Yesterday my feet had been scalded and cut. To-day they were covered entirely, top and sole with solid blisters. The scorching heat of the rocks under foot and of the surrounding atmosphere grew more and more intense. But Bill showed no mercy. His reason was soon clear. I had no water. The hours a white man can travel without water in such grilling heat are indeed few. Bill knew this. His watchful face was full of anxiety. The artist of our party had chosen to go on ahead of us, following the shore line of the lake; and old Thomasi, who carried his water bottle and mine and who feared for his safety, had followed him without giving us any warning.

But my own predicament seemed mild to me, when I suddenly became aware of the fact that little Bob was making the effort of his young life. Though he struggled painfully to keep up, he was constantly lagging behind and losing sight of us. His strong bare feet were torn and bleeding, and his smiling face had become serious. Until this morning, always eager to do more than his share, he had insisted on carrying my water bottle. To-day he had passed it over to old Thomasi, only when he had been told that he was slowing up the *safari*. Now he had taken off his spotted goat skin from his shoulders and had twisted it tight around his loins. He was an heroic little figure indeed, struggling along valiantly to keep up with the procession. His face was pursed up into an expression of suffering, but he never whimpered nor shed a tear.

Bill now emptied his last cup of water from his own small canteen, and Bob and I shared it. I left a quarter of a cup for Bill, but he would have none of it and made me finish it. Thus Bill urged us forward. We finally climbed up a high ridge, where graceful klipspringer leaped before us and unafraid stood watching our panting efforts. With all the world before them, I marveled that these little animals had chosen such a spot to dwell in. But they love a rocky solitude—it means safety—and here they had it. At last we gained the summit of the ridge and began the descent over the roughest, sharpest rocks we had yet encountered.

At the top of the rocky ridge our Kamasia guide suddenly pointed far away into the valley below. There, he told us, in a *donga* lined with green trees, we would find a little stream. The sight put new life into us. Hope now brought our strength and courage back! We moved on as quickly as possible. Bob limped along, leaving a little trail of blood wherever his wounded feet trod on a flat stone.

And just as the sun began to abate its fury a little, and the shadows deepened across the valley, we reached the green *donga*. All the boys plunged in to their knees and scooped the water up in their hands, drinking and laving their faces and bodies. No miser could have been more greedy over the sight of gold than we all were over the sight and possession of the far more precious water.

Ignoring all rules of the tropics, I drank from the stream. The water, which had run for miles under dense thorns and wild fig trees, was refreshingly cool and had a pungent, earthy taste like that of a New England brook after a spring rain. I drank sparingly, only enough to stop my burning thirst. Then I, too, waded in and splashed my clothing all over and soaked my hair in the stream. It was heavenly, just to be wet; I sat and rested in the first real shade I had seen for three days.

That night as I lay on my cot pitched in one of the few level spots among the rocks, I thought over the struggle of the day. I realized as I had many a time before how much responsibility, for our success and safety, Bill was continually taking. His burden was never light. It was his wisdom and his persistence and his watchful care which had brought us all through before fatigue overcame us. And as I lay there with the full, brilliant moon lighting the grim landscape around me, I could see my boys curled up in the crannies and crevices of the rocks and could hear only an occasional faint murmur of voices from the near-by stream where the Kamasia camp was outspread. They were all tired enough for sleep. No need to call to them, *"Bas kelele"* (Stop your noise!) that night.

It continued warm, but the wind was fresh. With my blistered feet bathed and bandaged in witch hazel, I rested comfortably and even slept a few hours. But poor little Bob, lying on a tarpaulin at the head of my bed, groaned all through the night. His sturdy little body was exhausted; the trip had been too hard for him, and I was very anxious about this child who had cast in his lot with mine.

The next day, when we finally reached the site we

Adventures in the African Jungle

had been seeking for our permanent camp, the poor youngster collapsed. I had my little tent put up for him, adjoining my own, and there for three days and nights he suffered the torments of high fever and delirium. I thought I was going to lose him, his temperature ran so high. I nursed him, relieving him by keeping him covered with a soaking bath towel, a method often used in fever cases.

Bob would not touch a mouthful of food, and I had to force him to drink and to take a little medicine. Accustomed as he was to the cool climate of Western Uganda, he did not recover his vigor during the time I was compelled to remain in the heat of Hannington. Nearly a month later, when the painting and accessories for the greater koodoo group were completed and I had to repeat my fifty-five mile journey to photograph the pink flamingoes at the head of the lake, I put Bob in the charge of Enoka, my cook, and sent them over a short route which we had finally discovered, a distance of only fifteen miles to the Evans' farm.

Back in Nairobi, many details had to be cared for, in order to finish the work of the expedition. Bob now became my constant companion. Everywhere I went in my motor car he accompanied me. He lugged all my heavy bundles from the market and the store. He waited on me in my room in our unfurnished stone house, set in its beautiful garden of fruit and flowers. He helped at table. He accompanied Bill and me in the motor truck when I had occasion to go out on the plains, and finally he journeyed with us to Bill's own *shamba* in the foot hills of Mt. Kenya.

He again begged for white man's clothes and I compromised by having my Goanese tailor make for him a short tunic in brown and red. Doubtless no child, native or white, was ever so dressed before, but it pleased me to have him wear a little 'coatee' as he called it and which I had designed especially to show his well developed chest and his lithe young arms and legs.

But I was always aware that Bob had never come back to normal health, even though we were again in a high altitude. I accordingly arranged that after my departure he should go to a local hospital for a few days of medical treatment. I also planned for his return to his own tribe, that he should go in care of the train conductor to Kisumu; that the ship's captain should care for him from Kisumu to Entebbe; that from there Captain Pitman, the game warden whom we had visited on our return from the Congo, should forward him by motor to Kabale; that Captain Tufnell should send him in care of a porter a three days' march back to his tribe. I was quite prepared to find that returning the child to his family was a more intricate undertaking than it had been to bring him on this long *safari,* but many a good friend came to my assistance.

Adventures in the African Jungle

When we had reached Nairobi, Bob had chosen to go with Bill into the servants' sleeping quarters, a building some distance away from the house which I now occupied alone. But one evening at twilight, three days before I was due to leave for America—and all the boys knew the time of my departure—Bob appeared at my door carrying his little red 'blanketty'—my old sun canopy. Without asking my permission, he unrolled it in one corner of the room and there made up his bed on the floor. He was weeping. I patted him on the shoulder. "What is the matter, Bob?" "Oh, *Memsahib*," he sobbed, "Never leave Africa. Stay here, here, here! Bob help you always." After this he clung to me closer than ever, helping me with my packing, running a hundred errands and always sitting with me on the front seat of the motor car. At intervals, he would stop and look at me while the tears welled up in his eyes. "*Memsahib*, no matter when you come back to Africa I shall always be waiting for you." Surely no one could ask of any human friend or vassal a greater fealty than came to me voluntarily from Bob's tender heart.

And as he stood with my black boys—a dozen of the old guard who had seen me through the year's *safari* and who came to the Nairobi station all dressed in their cleanest and best to see me off—my eyes as well as Bob's were filled with tears as I said good-by to him and to the land I had learned to love.

Adventures in the African Jungle

Bob—Mihigo, the Hunter, is now the only name he hears—reached his *shamba* on the 'Hill of the Lion' in safety. He is four years older now, taller, stronger, more nearly a man. His courage, too, has increased with his years and he will soon be unafraid to travel far alone. He is helping in the planting and the harvesting of peas and beans and bananas; he tends his father's flocks of goats and sheep and hump-backed cattle; occasionally he may carry a basket of ripe red strawberries on his head, porter fashion, to some weary English traveler who has paused for refreshment at the rest house at Kisola, with the blue Uganda mountains rising abruptly on the near horizon. Sometimes, too, he goes on *safari* with a white man, who easily may be astonished at the experience and aptness of the young native. My friend, Captain Tracy Philipps, the District Commissioner, sends me frequent messages from Bob. And from them I know that he remembers his promise: "*Memsahib*, no matter when you come back to Africa, I shall always be waiting for you."

THE JOYS OF AFRICA [1]

BY THEODORE ROOSEVELT

I SPEAK of Africa and golden joys, the joy of wandering through lonely lands, the joy of hunting the mighty and terrible lords of the wilderness, the cunning, the wary and the grim.

In these greatest of the world's great hunting grounds there are mountain peaks whose snows are dazzling under the equatorial sun, swamps where the slime oozes and bubbles and festers in the steaming heat, lakes like seas, skies that burn above deserts where the iron desolation is shrouded from view by the wavering mockery of the mirage, vast grassy plains where palms and thorn trees fringe the dwindling streams, mighty rivers rushing out of the heart of the continent through the sadness of endless marshes, forests of gorgeous beauty, where death broods in the dark and silent depths.

There are regions as healthy as the Northland, and other regions radiant with bright-hued flowers, birds and butterflies, odorous with sweet and heavy scents, but treacherous in their beauty and sinister to human life. On the land and in the water there are dread brutes that

[1] From Theodore Roosevelt's "African Game Trails"; copyright, 1909, 1910, by Charles Scribner's Sons. By permission of the publishers and the Roosevelt family.

[269]

Adventures in the African Jungle

feed on the flesh of man, and among the lower things that crawl and fly and sting and bite he finds swarming foes far more evil and deadly than any beast or reptile, foes that kill his crops and his cattle, foes before which he himself perishes in his hundreds of thousands.

The dark-skinned races that live in the land vary widely. Some are warlike, cattle-owning nomads; some till the soil and live in thatched huts shaped like beehives; some are fisher-folk; some are ape-like, naked savages, who dwell in the woods and prey on creatures not much wilder and lower than themselves.

The land teems with beasts of the chase, infinite in number and incredible in variety. It holds the fiercest beasts of ravin and the fleetest and most timid of those beings that live in undying fear of talon and fang. It holds the largest and the smallest of hoofed animals. It holds the mightiest creatures that tread the earth or swim in its rivers; it also holds distant kinsfolk of these same creatures, no bigger than woodchucks, which dwell in crannies of the rocks and in the tree tops. There are antelope smaller than hares and antelope larger than oxen. There are creatures which are the embodiments of grace; and others whose huge ungainliness is like that of a shape in a nightmare. The plains are alive with droves of strange and beautiful animals whose like is not known elsewhere, and with others even stranger that

Adventures in the African Jungle

show both in form and in temper something of the fantastic and the grotesque. It is a never-ending pleasure to gaze at the great herds of buck as they move to and fro in their myriads, as they stand for their noontide rest in the quivering heat haze, as the long files come down to drink at the watering places, as they feed and fight and rest and make love.

The hunter who wanders through these lands sees sights which ever afterward remain fixed in his mind. He sees the monstrous river horse snorting and plunging beside the boat, the giraffe looking over the tree tops at the nearing horseman, the ostrich fleeing at a speed that none may rival, the snarling leopard and coiled python with their lethal beauty, the zebras barking in the moonlight, as the laden caravan passes on its night march through a thirsty land. In after years there shall come to him memories of the lion's charge; of the gray bulk of the elephant, close at hand in the somber woodland; of the buffalo, his sullen eyes lowering from under his helmet of horn; of the rhinoceros, truculent and stupid, standing in the bright sunlight on the empty plain.

These things can be told. But there are no words that can tell the hidden spirit of the wilderness, that can reveal its mystery, its melancholy and its charm. There is delight in the hardy life of the open, in long rides, rifle in hand, in the thrill of the fight with dangerous game.

Adventures in the African Jungle

Apart from this, yet mingled with it, is the strong attraction of the silent places, of the large tropic moons and the splendor of the new stars; where the wanderer sees the awful glory of sunrise and sunset in the wide waste spaces of the earth, unworn of man and changed only by the slow change of the ages through time everlasting.

GLOSSARY

askari, soldier, sentry

baba, father
backsheesh, gratuities
banda, shed
baridi, cold
bas, stop
biltong, jerked meat
boma, post, government headquarters

chakula, food

dawa, medicine
donga, gulley
duka, shop

gongwa, sick

hapa, here
hema, tent, canopy
jambo, a greeting

kelele, noise
kiboko, whip of hippo hide, hippo
kikapu, little basket

Glossary

kopje, rocky eminence, literally "head"
kuja, come
kwenda, go

manyatta, a stockade or pen for cattle or sheep
memsahib, madam, mistress
mpagazi, porter
mpishi, cook
mshahara, wages

ndiyo, yes
neapara, head man
ngwena, crocodile
nullah, gulley
nyama, meat

panga, native knife, ax
piga, hurt
posho, daily ration, food money
pukka, proper

qua-heri, farewell, good night

safari, noun; outfit for travel in the field, including
     equipment and native employees
safari, verb; to make a trip or expedition into the field
sana, very great, very much
santa, thank you
shamba, field, plantation, garden
shenzie, low class native

Glossary

tembo, elephant
toto, baby, native boy, the young of any animal
tug, stream
twiga, giraffe

upesi, quick